Praise for *Naked!*

"If you want to find your perfect partner the natural and easy way, David Wygant is the man who knows how!"

— **Eddie Yu**, author of *Speedlights & Elephants: Winning the Online Business Game*

*"As a dating coach and participating member of the 'relationship club,' David Wygant strips away all the fantasy bulls$%t and clearly delivers the naked truth about relationships. **Naked!** is a great read. Ridiculously, hilariously, and refreshingly real!"*

— **Marni Kinrys**, *The Wing Girl Method*

NAKED!

ALSO BY DAVID WYGANT

Books

Always Talk to Strangers: 3 Simple Steps to Finding the Love of Your Life (available from all major booksellers)

The Fearless Code: Become a Natural with Women and Unmask the Authentic You (e-book)

Guy's Guide to Texting (e-book and audio program)

CD/DVD Programs for Men

The Art of Closing: How to Be a Great Dater (audio program)

Become a Master Communicator (audio and DVD program)

Become Her Sexual Fantasy: Unlock Her Secret Sexual Code (audio program)

Men's Mastery Series: The Complete Guide to Meeting Women (audio program)

No Excuses (audio program)

Own the Room: How to Create Success in All Aspects of Your Life (audio program)

Secrets of Online Dating (DVD program)

The Truth Behind What Women Desire in a Man

Undercover Approaches Women Crave: How Women Really Want Men to Approach Them (audio program)

CD/DVD Programs for Women

The Art of Attracting Men: The Inside Truth to the Way a Man's Mind Works (audio program)

No Excuses (audio program)

Women's Mastery Series (audio program)

All of the above are available at **www.davidwygant.com**.

NAKED!

How to Find the Perfect Partner by Revealing Your True Self

DAVID WYGANT

HAY HOUSE, INC.

Carlsbad, California • New York City
London • Sydney • Johannesburg
Vancouver • Hong Kong • New Delhi

Copyright © 2012 by David Wygant

Published and distributed in the United States by: Hay House, Inc.: www.hayhouse.com • *Published and distributed in Australia by:* Hay House Australia Pty. Ltd.: www.hayhouse.com.au • *Published and distributed in the United Kingdom by:* Hay House UK, Ltd.: www.hayhouse.co.uk • *Published and distributed in the Republic of South Africa by:* Hay House SA (Pty), Ltd.: www.hayhouse.co.za • *Distributed in Canada by:* Raincoast: www.raincoast.com • *Published in India by:* Hay House Publishers India: www.hayhouse.co.in

Editorial supervision: Jill Kramer • *Project editor:* Patrick Gabrysiak
Cover design: Amy Grigoriou • *Interior design:* Riann Bender

Library of Congress Cataloging-in-Publication Data

Wygant, David.
    Naked! : how to find the perfect partner by revealing your true self / David Wygant.
        p. cm.
    ISBN 978-1-4019-3397-5 (tradepaper : alk. paper) -- ISBN 978-1-4019-3398-2 1. Dating (Social customs) 2. Mate selection. 3. Man-woman relationships--United States. 4. Self-confidence. I. Title.
    HQ801.W94 2012
    646.7'7--dc23

                                    2011026942

ISBN: 978-1-4019-3397-5
Digital ISBN: 978-1-4019-3398-2

15 14 13 12   4 3 2 1
1st edition, January 2012

Printed in the United States of America

Thanks to all of my clients for allowing me to become a part of their lives. The work we do together has taught me more about life than I could ever learn by myself.

CONTENTS

Show me a dreamer who only dreams,

and I'll show you somebody who never achieves.

Show me a dreamer who not only dreams,

but applies himself every single day,

and I'll show you some of the most successful people in the world.

Doesn't matter if it's dating.

Doesn't matter if it's work.

Dreams alone won't get you anything but frustrated.

PREFACE

It may seem like an odd way to start a book, but here we go: Thank you.

Right about now you're probably asking yourself, *Thank you for <u>what?</u>*

Thank you for taking this very powerful step in order to reveal your true self and find the perfect partner. If you've been in the dating game for any amount of time at all, you know that most people put up walls that keep them from revealing their true selves to others. This book is all about breaking down those walls and cutting through the bullshit that gets in the way of building meaningful, long-term relationships.

Starting right *now*.

For more than 20 years, I've been earning the trust of men and women who are looking to transform their love lives. I have coached thousands of individuals on how to become more attractive to the opposite sex—in person and via my website, **www.davidwygant.com**. I write a weekly column for **AskMen.com**, I'm the head relationship writer for TangoWire (**www.tangowire.com**), and I post a blog several times a week on *The Huffington Post.* I've also made thousands of appearances in the broadcast, print, and online media, including *USA Today,* MSNBC, Playboy TV, ABC News, *Maxim, The New York Times,* Fox News, *Cosmopolitan, Inside Edition, Men's Health, Marie Claire,* MTV, *The Early Show,* and many more.

The story of how I became a dating coach is quite interesting. About 15 or 16 years ago, a friend and I were conducting a seminar together. It was about how to make money and how to market yourself. My friend kept telling me, "Do what you love, and the money will follow."

"Okay," I said. "That sounds great. But how does that bit of cosmic wisdom really work?"

He replied, "If you do what you love, you may not make money right away. But you'll stay true to who you are and be passionate about everything you do. And, like magic, you'll start getting clients. People are going to want to do business with you, because passion is contagious and everyone wants to feel it."

I thought about it, and I realized he was right. So I decided to become a dating coach. In the beginning, it was a little rocky; after all, you can't become something new overnight. It was an uphill battle for the first couple of years, but I stuck with it, and everything has worked out in a big way. There are those individuals in life who are fortunate to be able to do what they love, and I am lucky to be one of them. I truly believe that if you pursue your desires, the money will follow. And this is just what I teach all my clients: if you love and respect yourself, then the perfect partner will follow.

■ ■ ■

I spent my 20s and much of my 30s chasing money and women. I was very good at both. There was just one problem with this: I wasn't satisfied in my relationships. Every woman I decided to date was a carbon copy of the last one—and the last one wasn't very good. Why? Because I didn't learn the lesson the very first time and had to reconnect with the exact same person in a different body over and over again until I finally figured it out.

I used to look at meeting women as a game. To me it was a blast to be able to chase them, convince them that I was fantastic, and get a phone number. I always thought that the phone number was the conquest—the payoff. I really didn't understand the importance of self-love and creating the most powerful version of *me*.

Dating is really all about growing. Every person you meet is someone you get to know for a certain amount of time. During that period, you have a unique opportunity to learn more about yourself and what you want—in life and in a partner. Even if you've gone on 50 first dates and never been on a second one with the same person, you should just look at this as growth, where you can learn something about who you are while being in the company of another individual.

Have you ever had a relationship based on need? (Hasn't everybody had at least one or two?) For example, you're sick of being single, so you find the best possible person to be with at that time, even though you know he or she isn't right for you. At one point in my life I seriously considered marriage just because all my friends were getting married. Although I owned a bar in New York City—where there were plenty of women to chase—I was growing up, and I no longer wanted to be that guy chasing women every single weekend.

Sure enough, a good friend of mine decided that she'd fallen in love with me. So what did I do? I made it work. We broke up after three months, and things should have stayed that way. But I continued to pursue her, and we got back together and had a three-year relationship. She was a wonderful person, but we were honestly never aligned sexually or emotionally. We weren't even that great as lovers. We were just good friends, and it took three years for me to understand that.

During this process, though, I grew a lot. I realized that I have a high desire for passion and intimacy, and I need to be with somebody who has this same longing. And I accepted the relationship for what it was: a great, fantastic experience where I learned a lot about myself, as well as being close with another person. Dating is for growing, but getting to know yourself is the key.

When you enter any relationship, you need to get to know yourself so you don't repeat the same mistakes you made in your previous ones. However, it took me a while to figure that out. I would go out and chase women night after night, which continually yielded the same unfulfilling result. But here's a secret: when you're *chasing* a potential mate, you're not *attracting* a potential mate. Chasing is based on a need—a desire to be with somebody. Attraction, on the other hand, is rooted in the knowledge that there are plenty of people out there who are already attracted to you—you just haven't met them yet.

This mind-set change didn't happen to me until I was 37 years old. It was Thanksgiving, and I was at a friend's house for dinner. At this particular party, all the women were either in relationships or gay. I was frustrated. I wanted to meet someone. My friend's next-door neighbors were also throwing a party, so I walked over. The door was open, and I peeked in. A very pretty blonde was sitting there all alone, so I walked in and performed my standard chase routine. She loved it, and she gave me her number.

Mission accomplished.

I walked back to the party and told my friend, "I'm satisfied!"

She asked, "Really? Why?"

I told her what had just happened at the neighbors' house.

She then continued with her line of questioning: "That's great, but which version of you did she meet? The *real* version or the *comedic* version?"

At that moment, I understood exactly what she was talking about. I realized that I was always putting on an act—I was never just being *me*. I wanted to meet women and find a great girlfriend, but I wasn't being vulnerable and open. I wasn't being myself, I wasn't being natural, and it was a load of crap. I had created a performance, which is what potential mates saw the first time we met. And when you meet someone for the very first time, you automatically form opinions of each other, whether they're positive or negative.

So when you connect with people, and they harbor any small bit of doubt in their minds, that's the opinion they're going to carry with them when they go out on a date with you. It's difficult not to instantly form opinions, and once they're formed, they're extremely hard to alter. In fact, chances are that you may never have a chance to go back and change them. That's why so many individuals are on their very best behavior when they first meet potential mates. All they want to do is make sure that that this person likes them and has a positive impression of them.

The result of this, though, is that they present a watered-down version of themselves.

During the course of my many years of coaching men and women in how to transform their love lives, I've discovered that the root of failure in relationships is often a fear of honesty. We're fearful of being truthful with others, as well as with ourselves. In short, we're afraid to strip down and reveal to the world the naked truth of who we really are.

The only way you are ever going to meet somebody real—and build a genuine, long-term relationship—is by being the most powerful, amazing, and authentic version of *yourself.* Otherwise, when you try to create attraction with someone else, it's not going to be *real.*

So I decided that it was time to get real. And from that point forward, my connections were amazing. Even the sex I had was amazing. The dates I went on were so much fun, because I had no outcome in mind, and I didn't care which direction they went in. I just wanted to enjoy them and be myself. And if the women I went out with liked me, *great!* They liked me for who I really was, not because of some act I was putting on. And if they didn't like me, that was okay, too. The key was that I had an abundance mind-set: I knew that there were plenty of women out there who would like me.

And there were.

This new attitude led me directly to someone whom I had a fantastic five-year relationship with, and then ultimately to the wonderful woman I married. Today, I'm in the greatest relationship in the world with the most beautiful person I've ever laid eyes on—inside and out. I love her with all of my heart. By being in the moment, true to myself, and the most powerful version of myself, I am now living life as an abundant man who's full of love and completely unconcerned about what anybody else thinks.

I finally am who I am.

■ ■ ■

This book is going to strip you down to the core. This book is going to make you naked, like a little baby coming out of your mother's womb. This book is going to bring you back, even as it sends you forward. You are no longer going to care about the outcome of your dates or what other people think, because you're going to realize that you are just as you are right now: an amazing, beautiful, incredible individual who truly deserves to be with someone. Right now, you just haven't met him or her yet, and you haven't figured out how to do this.

When I'm done with you, you're going to know how to go out there and meet people. You're going to know how to cut through the bullshit and tear down the walls you've taken your entire life to build. And you're going to know how to let prospective mates meet the most powerful version of you.

In my experience, most daters have it all wrong. They're in the needy zone—desiring a relationship instead of knowing what you want before it even begins. When you learn how to create attraction for, and fall deep in love with, yourself—the real you—you'll understand that you have the ability to attract and meet people naturally. No longer will you ever need to go out chasing the excitement of the night in search of the party. You'll realize that you *are* the party.

And if there's one thing I've learned about the information I'm presenting to you in this book, it's that you'll not only date those you're most attracted to, you'll readily attract the kind of relationship you deserve as well.

And don't we all deserve at least that much in our lives?

I believe we do.

■ ■ ■

INTRODUCTION

Can You Handle the Truth?

One of my all-time favorite movies is *A Few Good Men,* starring Jack Nicholson and Tom Cruise. In that film, there's one scene in particular that just absolutely blows my mind. The famous part is when Tom Cruise has Nicholson on the stand in a military court of law, and Cruise's character is ranting and raving in an attempt to get Nicholson to tell the truth about what triggered the murder of a marine under his command. Finally, the lawyer screams, "I want the truth!"

Nicholson by then has had enough of Cruise's badgering. He erupts and yells back, "You can't handle the truth!"

That's a classic moment in film, and it's what this book is really all about: the truth. Can you handle the truth, or are you still looking at dating with unrealistic expectations? Are you simply dreaming, hoping that somebody will come into your life who is perfect for you in every possible way?

Notice the terminology that I'm using here: *dreaming* and *hoping.*

Everyone is different. Some people are just passive bystanders—waiting to see who randomly wanders into their lives—while others are active doers. Doers never dream and hope, they dream and *do.* And guess what? The only way you're ever going to actually meet that special someone is by getting off your ass and doing something about it. Doers make their own luck—they don't hope and pray for good fortune in finding their soul mate.

Now here's where I'm going to adapt Jack Nicholson's line from the movie and ask: Can *you* handle the truth? Are you ready to look back through your dating history and take the blame for everything that went wrong? Are you willing to forgive every relationship that backfired? Are you *truly* prepared to accept yourself 110 percent for who you are today—the good and the bad? Are you primed to be the real you—to live an honest life? More specifically, if trying to meet people in bars, nightclubs, and parties just isn't your thing, then are you ready to face the truth and do things differently?

■ ■ ■

I've had many women in my life. They've all been fantastic in different ways, and I've learned something from each one. You'll notice that I harbor no animosity about any of them. This is because I truly believe that the women who aren't datable would put it this way: "I've had a lot of crappy boyfriends. Men have cheated on me, and they've taken advantage of me. I've been used and abused my entire life. They're all a bunch of bastards." Or if a man were saying it: "It's ridiculous—I can't seem to find a girl who doesn't want me for anything more than my money. They're all just bitches."

But there's a very good (and simple) reason why those people who aren't datable have problems with getting into long-lasting, meaningful relationships: they're afraid to face their own truth. Their identity is based on fears and excuses, because they've never spoken about the men or women of their past in a positive way.

Remember for a minute how I talked about my past relationships. They were all amazing, with amazing people. When they didn't work out, it wasn't because the other people involved were bitches, or because they wronged me in some way. The relationships failed because we didn't share the same truth in what we wanted in life, and that was okay. I learned from them, and they learned from me. Of course, some of the relationships were more passionate than others, while some were better friendships. But they were *all* amazing.

Each woman I've been with has taught me something about myself—about who I was, who I am, and who I want to be. Relationships have so much to offer. Ultimately, it's how you embrace them when they end that makes you datable or not. I used to love when I went on a date and a woman would make a comment along the lines of, "I just don't trust men."

I'd look at her and say, "Well, you're not going to trust me, then, because I'm a man. So it was nice knowing you." And that was it for me.

But life is all about personal growth and digging deep inside. During the course of each of my relationships, I became naked, and I'm continually becoming more and more so. And that's why I wrote this book and titled it *Naked!* In fact, I'm naked right now: I'm vulnerable, raw, and experiencing things that I never have before. I've stepped outside of my comfort zone. But every day I need to become even more vulnerable and open so that I can experience more love.

To find the partner who's right for you, and with whom you can potentially spend the rest of your life, you've got to first face your own truth. You've got to accept it, and then you've got to live it. You need to be willing to be naked to the rest of the world. The more you understand how important this is, the more dating success you will have.

This book is all about getting you raw and open and helping you figure out what your truth is.

Who are you? What do you want? What do you need to experience? What have you not done so far? How far out of your comfort zone can you step? And once you've done so, how much farther can I bring you out of your comfort zone again? Are you ready to *really* get honest and forgive every single person who's ever wronged you in your life, especially when it comes to dating?

These are crucial questions, and they will make a tremendous difference in what kind of life you'll ultimately lead and how satisfied you'll be on a day-to-day basis.

■ ■ ■

In the chapters that follow, I'll first break you down and strip you naked. We'll tear away all the walls and barriers and protective mechanisms that you've constructed over the course of your life. Once we've taken care of the internal work—understanding the Law of Attraction in dating, discovering what you want in your life, getting in tune with what you're looking for in a mate, and more—then we'll turn our attention to external work. As we make this shift, we'll explore creating your own personal brand, making a video journal, navigating the world of online dating, and creating a plan for your life.

And to help put all this information into action, I have scattered numerous practical exercises throughout the book, which will play a critical role in your ultimate success. I strongly advise that you take the time to engage in each one, consider your results, and then incorporate your new discoveries into your own personal repertoire of basic dating techniques. Most of these exercises will require you to write in a journal or make lists, so be sure to have writing materials nearby.

You'll quickly find out that I'm a big fan of having you write about and make lists of things you want, the type of person you aspire to be, the kind of lover you want to find, and so on. Why do I have you do these tasks? Because you've got to learn how to manage your feelings, since they make you who you are.

In fact, I'd like you to do a bit of writing right now, which will help you start moving closer to your own truth. First, describe in detail the type of people you want to meet. Who are they? What are they all about? What do they look like? How tall are they? How short are they? How old are they? What do they like to do? Next, describe in detail who *you* are. What kind of person are you? What kind of mate are you looking for? What are you willing to give up in order to have a long-term relationship? What do you expect to receive in return? Right now, today, what is your truth?

Now I want you to think back at all the dates you've been on over the last year. Was there someone who you felt was just out of your league, and as a result you crashed and burned after going out just once? Did you ask way too much advice from friends about how to handle the situation? Or did you judge this potential mate before getting to know him or her?

Next, think about how you feel when you're emotionally naked. What type of feelings does this bring to the surface? Write them down. Do you feel fear? Excitement? Insecurity? Hope? I also want you to consider what it's going to be like when you meet Mr. or Ms. Right. How are you going to feel? How will you recognize that person? Are you ready to be 100 percent open with your partner?

Opening yourself up to meaningful relationships is all about getting vulnerable in every possible way. I want you to become so unguarded that you have no fears in life anymore. In fact, it's vital to understand that you're not born with fear, rejection, or disappointment. You learn all of these things; it's all social programming. You've been programmed to acknowledge these harmful emotions, and it's *you* who decides to experience them. My goal is to program your subconscious mind to no longer acknowledge them.

When you feel fear or rejection or disappointment, it's just your subconscious talking to you. If you objectively looked at that moment in reality, there's no reason for any of those feelings.

I've always told people that there's a difference between *real fear* and *fake fear*. In real fear, you're swimming in the ocean on a beautiful summer day. The sun is beating down, and you're floating among the waves. You realize that you've drifted out a little farther than you thought, but the sea is just so calm today. Then, all of a sudden, in the distance you see (what you think is) a black dot, but as it gets closer, you realize it's a fin. And now you've got 100 yards between you and that fin, and 50 yards between you and the shore. As it comes directly toward you, memories of *Jaws* come flying through your mind. That's real fear.

Fake fear is what you feel when you've got a date tomorrow night. You hope it works out but don't know what you're going to talk about. As the hour approaches, you get more and more nervous because you're drawing a blank on potential topics to discuss. You start calling your friends and asking them what you should say, what should you wear, and who you should be tonight. That's manufactured fear, and it doesn't do you any good. It creates walls between you and the man or woman who might be the person you've been dreaming about all your life.

As you take the journey I've laid out for you in this book, you're going to realize that you need to go out and meet that wonderful person. Because, when you get to the heart of what a first date is, you realize that it's just a chance to learn if you like someone and if he or she likes you. You don't need to sell yourself, be someone you really aren't, and go into the situation with fear. Real fear is floating in the middle of the ocean with the shark from *Jaws* chasing you back to shore. Fake fear is something you contrive yourself. And because you're the creator, you can stop it anytime you like.

Becoming naked is learning to trust your own instincts, refusing to give in to fear, and tapping into your real self. And it's all about staying completely open and communicating your reality to others—and also being open when someone communicates his or her reality to you. I know that this isn't an easy thing to do, but it can be done. I'll show you how to become naked and, therefore, the person you were always meant to be. As a result, you *will* attract the right relationship for you, with someone you can spend the rest of your life with.

In the first chapter of this book, we'll begin by considering how obsessing about what our dates think about us can cause us to miss out on opportunities that we should be embracing.

■ ▦ ■

CHAPTER 1

THE ARTICLES OF OBSESSION

I might be dating myself a little bit here, but what's a few years among friends, right? For those of you who are old enough to remember a rock-and-roll singer by the name of Meat Loaf, you will also surely recall his hit song "Paradise by the Dashboard Light." If you don't happen to be familiar with it, the song is all about a guy who's debating whether or not he'll sleep with a woman. She seems to be game, but only if he's willing to tell her that he'll love her forever. The problem is, he's just not sure he's ready to do that.

Meat Loaf tells the woman that he's going to need to sleep on it and then let her know the answer in the morning. On the one hand, he's driven to tell the woman whatever she needs to hear to allow him to sleep with her. But on the other hand, Meat Loaf is afraid to make any sort of long-term commitment—no matter how much he desires her. (Well, he did sleep on it, and then he promised to love her to the end of time—a decision he soon came to regret.)

And then there's that famous (or maybe I should say *infamous*) film *Animal House*—you might remember that one, too. The scene I'm thinking about is when the character played by Tom Hulce, freshman Larry Kroger, is confronted with a dilemma while he's trying to hook up with the mayor's daughter. You see, she gets falling-down, shit-faced drunk and passes out in his bed. And if that isn't bad enough, all the stuffing in her bra comes out and he realizes she's underage.

Kroger quickly realized that not only did the subject of his ardor "enhance" her appearance with toilet paper—a major game changer in itself—but she was completely unconscious. Thus began the internal debate that would seal his fate. On his right shoulder, the devil was demanding that he have sex with her right *now*. On his other side, the angel was trying to convince him to avoid the temptation. The result was conflicting advice, just like in the Meat Loaf song. Larry Kroger eventually decided to do the right thing, and he took his date home where he left her untouched and unharmed at the front door of her home . . . in a shopping cart.

Now let's talk about *your* life and the conflicting advice that you have to deal with every day.

When you're wondering about your dating issues—whether it's why your date didn't call back or what he or she is thinking—do you go into re-engagement mode? In other words, do you go to one or more of your close friends and ask them questions like:

- What do you think he meant when he said that?

- Do you think she's going to call?

- How do you think I should play this thing?

- What do you think I should do in this situation?

- What would *you* do in this situation?

- She said this on the date. How should I interpret that?

People do this to me all the time—I have clients who call me and try to re-engage. I'll quickly interrupt them and ask, "Will you please just stop this madness? I don't know what they said or what they're thinking—I have no idea. Why don't you give me their phone number, and I'll call to find out exactly what they meant." The person on the line gets my message at this point, which is that it's no use speculating what a date meant by a comment he or she made.

My advice is always the same no matter who asks me to guess someone else's intentions. I'll say, "If you love who you are, then why don't you go and sit down with this person and find out what they meant? If it's bothering you that much, then you owe it to yourself and to your future relationships to resolve this issue."

Here's a recent example. I was working with a client who felt that she was no more than a booty call for the guy she was dating, and she wanted more. He'd see her when it was convenient for him, but then wouldn't make her a priority if he had anything else going on. She asked me over and over again, "What do you think this means?"

"What it sounds like is that this person doesn't want to commit to you," I told her. "But if you *really* want to know where you stand with him, then you need to confront him face-to-face. *Nobody* can give you accurate advice on what another person is thinking unless the two of them have sat down and had a conversation."

She followed my advice and discovered that the guy wasn't interested in committing to a long-term relationship. Armed with that information, my client broke it off with him and found someone else.

All of us have a third-base coach when we're out looking for a mate—someone we can talk about our dating issues with. Some of us may even have an entire coaching *staff* supporting us: a tight-knit group of friends, college buddies, work associates, relatives, neighbors, or other well-wishers. While it's great to have the help of so many people who want nothing more than for us to find someone who will make us happy for the rest of our lives, so much of our talk about relationships just goes around and around, never getting us anywhere.

Again, the root of the problem is that your date is the only person who can tell you what he or she is thinking.

When we engage anyone else—"What do you think it meant when he did that?" "What do you think I should do right now?" "What do you think I should say the next time she does this?"—we're really showing that the problem isn't with the other person, but it's with *us*. The only reason we bring outside influences into the process and ask them to try to guess the intentions of someone else is because we're afraid to get raw, become vulnerable, and face the truth.

Think about it. If you find yourself asking a friend these questions or others like them, why in God's name do you continue to do this? In my experience, it's because you're scared of *really* knowing what your date thinks, and you'd much rather be stuck in a sea of perpetual confusion.

When it comes right down to it, people are frightened to voice how they truly feel to the individuals they care about. Why? Because they believe that if they say something that might offend or hurt someone they care about, that person won't love them or want to be with them anymore. Rather, they prefer to be somebody's human punching bag instead.

In dating, it's important—actually, it's *critically* important—for you *not* to re-engage your friends over and over again in circular talk. For you to grow, you've got to become vulnerable and naked, dig deeply for the truth, and sit face-to-face with the person you're dating to find out what he or she is really thinking.

■ ■ ■

Are you a *rehasher?*

No, not somebody who orders eggs and hash browns at the local diner, takes them home, and then rehashes them the next morning. The kind of rehashing I'm talking about is people who will go out on a date—maybe a few dates—and then if the relationship suddenly fizzles out, they drive their friends crazy for the next two weeks as they relive and replay every single moment: "If I just said this." "If I just did that." "If he would have just reacted to me in this way." "It was over all because I didn't react in that way. That's why we're not going out again!"

All of this rehashing is ridiculous, and it's a big waste of your time and energy. It's not the one thing you did or didn't do that killed your relationship. It's a combination of things—energy, chemistry, and timing, to name a few. There's so much more involved than just one stupid little thing that you could've done better. Usually, nothing you could have done would have saved the situation anyway.

So if you're driving your friends crazy rehashing your last failed date 24/7 over something that you think might have gone wrong, stop it! Maybe life at that moment was throwing you a curveball. Maybe the other person had things going on in his or her life. Maybe you had things going on in yours. Whatever it was, what's done is done. So stop rehashing the past, and start focusing on finding Mr. or Ms. Right.

A client of mine once told me about a fantastic six-hour date that he claimed was the experience of a lifetime. At the end of the night, he gave the woman a hug and told her how much he enjoyed spending time with her. He then called her the very next day and left a message. He told her how he'd had a wonderful time the day before and that he hoped he would see her again soon.

But guess what? She never called him back.

So what do you think my client did next? He started overthinking and overanalyzing *everything.*

All of his self-doubts and insecurities began to spew uncontrollably from his mouth. He then began a post-date recap, breaking down every conversation that occurred that night and wondering if he'd said something that might have turned her off. Maybe she didn't think he was sexually attracted to her because he didn't kiss her at the end of the night. If he had just given her a kiss, things would have turned out much differently, right?

My client wanted an immediate coaching session with me to rehash everything that had gone on during the course of his six-hour marathon date. About 15 minutes into the conversation, I said, "Stop! This is madness. Give me your phone—right now."

Immediately, he handed over the phone. I found her number, turned on the speaker, and pressed CALL. He quickly grabbed the phone and screamed, "What are you doing?!"

I replied, "I'm ending your misery. The answer doesn't lie with me. I can't tell you what you want to hear. I don't know who she is or why she didn't call you back. But what I do know is that you're driving yourself crazy, and this self-torture isn't going to work. The *only* way to find out why she didn't call you back is to ask."

He looked at me for a moment and then responded, "David, that's so wrong. Won't I come across to her as needy? Isn't that needy? I'm going to look needy to her, right?"

I countered: "Look needy in front of who? What do you care? Don't you want to know why she hasn't called you back?"

"But she's going to lose all respect for me!"

"You have no respect for yourself," I told him. "So you'd rather torture yourself, engage all your friends in circular talk for the next two weeks, and obsess about her. And during this time, there's not a chance in hell that you're going to meet anybody else, because you'll be in obsession mode. And when you're in this state, you won't be open to any new opportunities. Self-torture does nothing but cause you stress. You're not going to benefit from it. The only thing you'll learn from is calling this woman again and finding out why she never got back to you."

My client looked at me like I'd just climbed out of a spaceship in the Hollywood Hills and said to him, "ET phone home."

After a few seconds, he finally spoke. "Well I can't do that. I'm going to look needy."

By this time I was about to punch the guy to try to knock some sense into him. But I resisted the temptation and made one more attempt to get through to him. "This is the most ridiculous thing in the entire world. Why the hell does it matter that you're going to look needy? Do you think that if you ask her what she's thinking, she's going to paste it all over Facebook or Twitter that you're a needy guy? After all, you two just had a fabulous six-hour date! Do you honestly believe she'll tell the world that some guy called her and asked why she didn't call him back? Do you care that much about other people's opinions of you? Do you have so little respect for yourself that you care more about what others think than what *you* think about yourself?"

I continued, "So you know what? Why don't you go ahead and stay in this self-destructive mode. I've got no problem with that. I'll sit here. We can book hour after hour, and I can simply take your money as you torture yourself and search for the answers. I may even say something that makes you feel better for 20 minutes after our session—until you go back into self-torture mode again.

"But I'm going to end this right now by making you call her, because we have no idea what she's thinking. Let's grow as a person. Let's call her right now, put her on speaker, and find out the truth."

At this point, I was actually surprised when he took out his phone and hit the CALL button.

The phone rang, and his date picked up. "Hello?" she answered.

"Hi, Amy. It's Steve. How are you doing?"

"Oh my God, Steve, I am *so* sorry for not calling you back!" she apologized. "I was hoping you would call me. I lost my phone soon after I listened to your voice mail. I lost all my numbers and messages. Thank God you called me back!"

On the other end of the phone, I heard her sigh. She then proceeded, "That was one of the best dates I've ever had. It's funny, I've been talking to my friends about this for the last ten days, saying to them, 'Is he going to call again? He probably thinks I blew him off. I really liked him. Maybe he wasn't that in to me.'"

As my client's date revealed her own self-torture mode, the two of them shared the fears they had gone through for the last week and a half, laughing about it together.

I'm happy to report that Amy and Steve went on another great date, and they've been a couple ever since.

Of course, your own results may be different. You may call someone up, and he or she may say, "I'm not interested in you," "I don't feel the same way you do," or "I just want to be friends." Believe it or not, that's okay, since it doesn't matter what happens. At least you know the truth. You can then move forward with your life and avoid the self-torture mode altogether. Trust me, you've got nothing to lose and everything to gain by having some guts and getting some closure. It just takes a simple phone call, e-mail, or text message.

That's it.

And one more thing. Besides bringing closure— whether it's good news or bad news—this gives you the self-respect you need to be the healthy, fully functioning adult you are.

Poor Steve would have beaten himself up for weeks . . . maybe even months or years. And if he ran into Amy again on the street, in a grocery store, or at Starbucks— which would likely happen eventually—he probably would have tried to hide.

The game of adult hide-and-seek just kills me, but it happens all the time. Here's how it's played: When you're in, say, a store and you see someone you went on a date with but who never called you back, you look down at the floor and pretend you didn't notice that person. Or you both look at each other and do "distance looking": where you look beyond the other person and "don't see" him or her, not acknowledging the fact that you really did see each other.

But Steve didn't have to play adult hide-and-seek, and his life is all the better because he decided to find out why his date didn't return his call. Making the tough calls is what becoming naked is all about. If you can do this in the beginning, then when you're mistreated in a relationship (yes, it does happen), you're able to sit down with somebody and speak from your heart, which will cause him or her to do the same.

■ ■ ■

Here's another real story—this time from one of my female clients.

I was working with a really great woman from New York who had met a guy she was interested in having a long-term relationship with. The man was a little older than she was; and he was powerful, strong, and successful. They went out on one date, and she felt really good being around him. He was the sexy, debonair, confident guy that my client liked. He'd also been married a few different times, which made him seem as if he knew where he was in his life. Needless to say, this woman was very emotionally and physically turned on by him.

She asked me: "How do I charm this man? He's very sexual." With my help, she started engaging him sexually—flirting with him via text messages, sending him pictures, and e-mailing him seductive notes. She was matching what she thought was his sexual energy, and having a lot of fun in the process.

There was just one problem, and it was a major one: He wasn't able to satisfy or match her energy. As a result, she started getting very frustrated. "He went down to Florida for a week or two and didn't invite me to join him. He goes to a business meeting and decides to hang out with his work buddies or clients at a bar afterward, but he forgets to call me. What's he thinking? What do I do?"

You can probably guess by now what I told her. "I have no idea, but I do know that he doesn't deserve you. If a man refuses to give you what you need—sexually or emotionally—then you don't need to stick around. You've got two options: either you look your date directly in the eye and find out the truth, or you walk away."

Believe it or not, life really is that simple, and we've overcomplicated it in so many different ways. We're afraid of the truth—like Jack Nicholson said, "You can't handle the truth!" We're afraid to talk about what's on our minds and get naked, so we let issues build until they kill any chance of having a healthy relationship.

Long story short, my client let the situation with this guy linger for weeks. So every day her disappointment grew a little more. He didn't call. He didn't invite her on a trip. And he didn't even acknowledge Valentine's Day!

I finally told her, "Listen, this guy's treating you as a booty call, and that's it. You deserve so much more. Why do you think you're going to get him to change? There's no game you can play. He is who he is. He's not emotionally able to give to you. Playing some trick to get him to start giving you what you need just isn't going to work. It never will. You're holding on to a dream and an illusion of a fantasy that you've come up with in your head. You must learn when to let go and move on."

I'm proud to say that she followed my advice and stopped obsessing about him. Within a month, she found someone else who happened to be exactly the kind of person she'd been dreaming about and hoping for all along.

■ ■ ■

Before you move on to the next chapter, you've got to fully comprehend this lesson and begin—right *now*—to live it yourself.

Understand that the answer does not lie with your group of friends, your advisors, your parents, your boss, your coaches, or whoever else you might run to whenever you have a dating problem. The answer lies in the person you went out with. If you're hung up on somebody and don't know what they're thinking, then get on the phone and call them. If they don't pick up, leave a message.

Here's a short script you can use to craft your own conversation:

Hi Mary,

It's David. There's something I'm curious about and need to ask you, and only you can help me out with it. I really had a great time at dinner with you last week. I called you to set up another date and never heard back. I just need to know why. I'm interested in you. Are you interested in me? If so, great— let's talk about it. If not, no worries. Let's talk about that, too. I just need to know one way or the other.

Being able to communicate and find out things for yourself is going to teach you how to believe in what your own gut and intuition are telling you.

Now, I'm not saying never go to friends for advice or never hire a dating coach like myself. I'm trying to get you to trust yourself more fully and learn how to have those tough conversations. This will allow you to grow as a person and ultimately find the love you deserve.

■ ■ ■

Here's an exercise I'd like you to do right now.

Write down all the missed opportunities that you've had over the past year to call somebody back. I want you to include all of the individuals that you obsessed about with your friends. Next to each name, I want you to write down how much time you spent consumed by him or her. Was it a day? A week? Two weeks? A month?

After that, add up the total hours you've spent obsessing in the last year. What number did you get? This is the time you could have been meeting other people. How long would it have taken for you to simply pick up the phone and call the person one more time and find out the truth? I can guarantee that number is small potatoes compared to the hours you wasted.

Falling in love with yourself and becoming naked and vulnerable means that you're going to have to get answers for yourself. So the next time somebody drives you crazy, what are you going to do?

In the next chapter, we'll explore the Law of Attraction in dating, and how you can use it to your advantage.

■ ▇ ■

CHAPTER 2

THE LAW OF ATTRACTION IN DATING

Most people today are familiar with the idea of the Law of Attraction. But in case you've been hiding under a rock for the past 10 years, however, its basic definition is simply this: *like attracts like.* That is, if you put out positive energy, you'll get positive energy back in return. And if you put out negative energy, then—guess what?— you'll get negative energy right back.

In my many years of working with individuals who are trying to attract the kind of relationships they want in their lives, I find that they usually understand the Law of Attraction but don't really live it.

I've always been an entrepreneur and had lots of different businesses. I've worked for myself, I suppose, since

I was about 26 years old. The problem is that for the first ten years or so I was always chasing money, deals, businesses, and customers. I was chasing the chase.

And during that time, I was also chasing women.

I was going out all the time in an attempt to meet the opposite sex. I'd wake up on a Saturday morning and think, *Where can I go find women today?* I wasn't doing what I love or creating the amazing lifestyle that we have touched on so far in the book (and will get into even deeper in the chapters that follow). I simply chased.

I distinctly remember one time when I lost money in a particular business venture. I couldn't figure out what had gone wrong. Everything was in place to make money—the right idea, the right pitch, the right product. But for some reason, it was a big loser. And then a friend pointed out that I wasn't practicing the Law of Attraction with money and was lacking a mind-set of abundance.

I remember asking my friend, a bit irritated, "What am I supposed to do? Stand here and repeat over and over, 'I am abundant, I am abundant, I am abundant!'?"

My friend looked at me and replied, "Yeah, that's exactly right. You're supposed to say that over and over again. No matter what part of your life you're saying it for—dating, money, your career, sex—it could be anything. Whatever it is, you've got to say it repeatedly, and you've got to believe it. And once you believe it, then you've got to live it."

"Okay, well how do I live it?" I asked.

And that's really the big question when it comes to the Law of Attraction: how do you live it in your everyday life? The secret is to first understand what it means in a dating context.

As I mentioned at the beginning of this chapter, the Law of Attraction says, in essence, that like attracts like. So, when it comes to dating, this means that you will attract those individuals whom your own personality, attitude, and energy projects to the world around you. And it's true—I've seen this idea play out time and time again.

■ ■ ■

I had a client one time who was a really wonderful man. In fact, he was without a doubt the nicest man I've ever coached. He was wondering why he would always attract needy women—he just couldn't figure it out. All the women he was interested in had this quality in one way or another. Sometimes they were needy with money, sometimes they were needy for affection, or sometimes they were needy at work. As desperate as he was to find someone who didn't express neediness, it was almost guaranteed that anyone this man dated was going to possess this quality.

So I looked at my client and asked, "Have *you* ever been needy before?"

He immediately got defensive. "Me, needy? No way."

I pushed a bit more. "Come on, now—let's be honest here. At any point in your life have you ever been needy in the same way the women you've been dating have been with you?"

After a moment, he admitted, "Yes, there are times when I've been needy about money, affection, and sex. I remember this point in my life when I was really needy about money. My business was slow to the point of me wondering if it was going to succeed. It had been doing well for a few years, then all of a sudden it started to go downhill, and as a result I became very afraid. And it seemed that the more desperate for money I became, the less I had coming in."

My client continued, "There was another time in my life when I was coming off of a bad relationship with a woman who was very unaffectionate, and I remember asking myself, *Am I ever going to meet another affectionate woman again?* While I was single and looking for a girl-friend, I wanted affection so bad, yet I couldn't seem to attract anyone who would reciprocate."

"So what was it about your being needy for sex?" I inquired.

"I've got a high sex drive," my client told me, "but it seemed like I was always with women who didn't. So my focus during the course of a typical date was to try to figure out what kind of intimacy level my potential partner had. Would her idea of romance match mine, or would I be disappointed again? I tried to find a way to ask the person about lovemaking and what she liked, and at that moment she would want to get up and leave the table. When I was really needy about sex, I never ended up sleeping with any of the women I dated. Just like the money I was so desperate for and never got, and just like the affection I was so starved for and never got, I was stressed out about never having sex."

"During those times in your life, were you dating anybody?"

"Oh, absolutely," he replied.

"Do you see what the Law of Attraction did? You were needy, so it attracted another needy person. You attract-ed someone with your own personality," I pointed out.

The lesson for this guy wasn't that he needed to stop dating these types of women. It was that *he* needed to stop being needy and start being self-sufficient.

I'm not saying that you need to hold back from desiring or wanting somebody, or that you don't need anyone to be affectionate, loving, or caring toward you. That's got nothing to do with it at all. It's all about how needy you are, about wanting something so bad and pushing hard for it. It's amazing. When you're needy, you attract another needy person, and it may not even be in the same way that you are. For example, you may require a lot of affection, and your date may want words of affirmation. She might need to hear repeatedly that she's the most beautiful woman in the world.

To that end, I had a client one time who was an absolute knockout, and she also happened to be incredibly sexy, successful, sweet, and loving—just an all-around great person. If you saw her on the street, you'd never think she had any insecurities or self-doubts, but she did. Big time. She told me that she'd had many bad relationships, and the reason was because the men she dated didn't understand her.

"Did you help them understand you?" I asked.

Her response was, "I tried. They just didn't understand my needs."

I knew what this woman really wanted: a man to tell her how beautiful she was, and not just once every other month. She longed to hear it every day. Of course, we all love to hear how sexy and beautiful we are. But what makes this great is when someone is actually feeling it and doing it based on the love and desire and passion that's been established in the relationship. And if someone needs to hear it over and over and over again, then they're being very needy.

So I inquired, "Do *you* think you're beautiful?"

"Maybe not," she replied. "I think that's why I always need to hear it."

Do you see where I'm going with this story? If this remarkably gorgeous woman thought she was beautiful—and was really confident about it—then she wouldn't have attracted the needy men who were keeping her from having a satisfying, long-term relationship.

Here's a secret: If you're 100 percent self-sufficient—if you get out of bed every day, are satisfied and positive about your life, and think you're attractive—then that's the energy you're going to put out to the rest of the world. And you know what? People will feel that energy and respond to it . . . and it won't be the needy ones. Those who are going to notice will also be fulfilled and positive about their lives and think they're attractive, too. This is true if it's your first encounter with a person or if you've been dating somebody for a long period of time.

So here's the deal. If you walk around frustrated and negative about your life, and you put that energy out there to the world, then that delightful, gorgeous person that I just talked about isn't going to get anywhere near you at all. Not a chance. What will happen instead is that you'll attract potential mates who are unhappy and dissatisfied. You'll find exactly who you are.

■ ■ ■

The Law of Attraction in dating is powerful stuff. When I had a particular lesson to learn during some stage of my life, I always seemed to come upon the kind of person who could teach it to me. And if for some reason he or she couldn't help me, then someone else would be there who could. And this would happen over and over again until finally I gained the knowledge I was supposed to.

What was the lesson? I'm glad you asked, because it was about confidence.

I was attracting mates who had insecurities. Everybody has self-doubt about something, but for some reason I was meeting women who were overly vulnerable about their sexuality and themselves. I, in turn, was very secure about my sexuality, but not about *myself.* I was going through a period of my life where I was trying to find who I was. There were many days when I'd wake up with doubts about my identity. I honestly didn't know how to define myself.

And when you're dating the mirror image of yourself, you're going to end up being immensely frustrated— you're going to drive yourself *crazy*. You can easily get along with someone when everything is going great and clicking. But the second dissatisfaction or neediness of any kind comes up between two people who are so alike, issues start rising to the surface.

Now, I realize that there are frustrations and arguments in every relationship. There are even disagreements within yourself if you think about it. But what happens when you're not completely in tune with your emotions and who you are is that you end up hiding some part of yourself from other people. And when you do that, you'll attract somebody who's also holding something back.

So the next time you look at others and they're broadcasting those telltale needy signals, you've got to look deeper into it. Ask yourself, "Why did I attract this person in the first place?"

The answer is actually quite simple. It's because there are things that you still haven't mastered about yourself. This goes much deeper than just projecting negative energy. Even when you're a well-formed person and have done a lot of work on yourself, you'll still attract the wrong people, butt heads with them, and go through periods of learning lessons. So, when you're dating somebody who frustrates you, you always have a choice. You can stick with a bad situation and continue to make the wrong decisions over and over again, or you can step back, take a look at yourself, and change.

Try this the next time you're at odds with someone you're dating. Tell him or her, "Listen, I think we need to be more loving and affectionate with one another. We would really benefit from creating that environment together, because we both really deserve this and need it in order to be happy together."

Think about how that sounded: it was positive, it was beautiful, and it acknowledged that you made a huge realization—you attracted this person into your life so you could learn a lesson. You could be a fantastic, amazing, and satisfied person, but when you get romantically involved with somebody, there is always going to be something that you need to learn. So by understanding that, you can change the words and the attitude from "*I* really need *you* to be more affectionate and loving" to "*We* really need to be more affectionate and loving."

What I want you to do right now is practice this. While this book is all about reformulating yourself—stripping yourself down to become naked to the point that you'll be so open and vulnerable when you meet the next person in your life that it's going to be an incredible experience—keep in mind that you're still going to have issues to resolve in any relationship, no matter how great it is.

Here's another script you can practice. Instead of saying something like, "I really hate it when you're cheap. I can't stand it. It makes me feel so uncomfortable." You can flip it upside-down: "Listen, when we go out, we really need to be more generous. We should never be cheap with ourselves, because we're going to rip ourselves off from some amazing opportunities and experiences together." It's much more powerful to use "we" instead of "you," because it focuses on the relationship and doesn't place blame on either person.

■ ■ ■

Okay, it's time for another exercise.

Get out a piece of paper and a pen and think about someone you dated in the past but no longer go out with. Next, make a list of the things that really irritated you about that person—the things that make your blood boil. Why am I asking you to do this? Because practicing how to communicate is going to help you attract the right person—another communicator who is working on him- or herself, too. Who knows, maybe they've even read this book and really understand the depth of who they are.

Continue to write down all the irritating things you can think of that your ex did. Get creative and have fun with it. Now I want you to rephrase each of the irritating items on your list by taking every *I* and turning it into a *we*, just like I demonstrated a few paragraphs earlier.

Okay? Ready for the next step? Good.

First, I want you to go into attack mode. Say, "*I* really need you to be more loving," "*I* really need us to have more sex," or whatever it is that irritated you. Return to that place in your mind when you were angry with this person, and be sure to exclusively use the pronoun *I*.

Now I want you to look in the mirror, or, if you're really gutsy, sit in front of a camera and film yourself, because that will be even more powerful. But let's assume for the moment that you decided to do this exercise in front of the mirror. I want you to attack that mirror as if you're attacking your ex. Say, "*I* really can't stand the fact that we don't have enough sex!" Really get into the pain you felt at the time—really feel it.

Notice what you see looking back at you. Memorize your facial expression, and then ask yourself this question: Would *you* be attracted to yourself, or would you react with defensiveness and attack?

After you finish this first round of the exercise, I want you to start round two. Rephrase each statement in an incredibly nice way, using the pronoun *we*. Say, "*We really need to be more loving with one another," "*We should make a point of having more sex," or whatever you said in the first part.

Then, look at yourself again in the mirror. What does your expression say now? How would *you* feel if someone came at you in that way? When someone is pleasant, relaxed, open, and inviting, he or she is far more attractive than a person who's mad, agitated, or confrontational. It's simply a much more attractive situation for anyone.

This exercise is designed to help you understand who you are, and it really works.

Ready for round three? Good. Next, think, *Am I positive? Am I willing to compromise? What are my priorities?*

Now, I want you to write down what you stand for. What are your priorities? Are you generally positive? Do you wake up in the morning and truly believe that every day is the gift that it is? Become aware of what you project to others around you.

Are you always wondering why you don't attract anybody or meet people who you're interested in? If you're someone who's addicted to your BlackBerry (there's a reason why it's nicknamed a *Crackberry*) or iPhone, this might be because you're so obsessed with the latest technology that you never "see" the individuals in your life. The number one antisocial tool in the world is your smartphone (or, as I call it, *dumb* phone). The more time you spend on yours, the less you're going to be attracting who you want in your life.

■ ■ ■

Here's yet another great exercise for you to do. Have a friend follow you around one day as you go through your normal routine, taking photographs or videos of you all along the way. After you return home, sit down and analyze what was captured. How do you look in public? What do you project to others? Are you happy, or do you appear sad and miserable? Do you give the impression of being fun and appealing? Do you stand out from the crowd, or do you blend in because you never smile?

How about when you were in the grocery store shopping for food? Did you rush through the aisles, not noticing anyone and never taking the time to smile? Did you go in there distracted and thinking about work? When you're not fully in the moment, you're not going to be able to attract anybody. The next time you visit your favorite places, make it a point to be totally present. It could be in a bar, a restaurant, a coffee shop, a bookstore, the beach, or wherever you like to hang out. These are all places that you're going to be meeting potential dates once you understand the Law of Attraction.

Understand that you command attention wherever you go—people look at you, and they form an immediate impression. If their first instinct is that you're not interesting, then you won't create attraction.

But we're not done yet.

Go out the very next day and repeat this exercise. Don't wait a week or a month. Get out there *the very next day*. Have a friend follow you around with a camera again, but now approach things in a different way. As you go through your regular routine, smile, say hello to people, enjoy the day, and be really positive. Now head back to your place and check out the results.

If you did this right, you'll see people noticing you. Your positive energy will *always* bring positive people to you, and negative energy will *always* repel them. This is a huge first step in creating attraction.

■ ■ ■

Here's a terrific exercise I do during my boot camps that's all about positive energy. I'll get a group of participants together and send them to a local grocery store. Before I do so, however, I'll make sure it's a location where I can look through the window and easily observe what's going on inside.

I split the group into two halves and direct the first group to go into the store with sour, miserable looks on their faces. I'll even have some of them partake in blatantly antisocial behaviors, such as playing with their phones. Then I'll have the other half of the group observe what happens from the outside and ask them if they notice anything interesting.

And they always do.

During this approximately five-minute exercise, the observation group will pick up on some very significant behaviors: shoppers walk in the other direction when they see the despondent boot campers coming at them, go out of their way to avoid them, and give them lots of dirty looks. This is an amazing thing to watch, because it becomes clear that energy really is everything.

So after the first group's time is up, I'll pull them out of the store and get the observers ready to take their place. But instead of walking in looking miserable, I instruct these individuals to go in smiling, as if they're enjoying everything about the market. I tell them to act like everything they see—the bread, the peanut butter, the stinky cheese—is the greatest thing they've ever laid eyes on. I then have the members of the sour-faced group watch from outside, and the difference is incredible.

While the new shoppers walk through the store smiling, admiring the food, and giving off great energy, they have the exact opposite effect on those they interact with than did the earlier, sour-faced group. The other customers are actually *attracted* to them—they smile back, move closer, and engage in conversations. There's even some flirting here and there.

The lesson? It's all about your energy. Positive energy is contagious, but so is negative energy. When someone sneezes near you, what's your normal reaction? Do you hold your breath? Or what happens if someone coughs on an airplane? You probably cover your face with a tissue, go to the bathroom and wash your hands, or you wince.

Well, spreading germs is the same as spreading negative energy. When someone goes into a store and is visibly angry with a scowl on his or her face, *nobody* wants to catch that.

■ ■ ■

So what type of relationship do you desire next? One that's positive, amazing, and loving? You can have all that. Once you understand the Law of Attraction in dating and learn to create with it, you'll start meeting the most intriguing people. How do I know? Because not only have I coached clients for years on how to do so, but I've been doing it myself on a daily basis, since they're the only types of individuals I want in my life.

Here's one last story for you to consider. A man came to me one time and said, "I only attract gold diggers—it's unbelievable. They ask me for rent money. One even asked me for new car—on the second date! Have you ever had a woman ask you that?"

I replied, "Never in a million years has a woman asked me to do any of those things. I only attract really incredible, beautiful, interesting people. Do you want to know why you're attracting that type of person? Because you drive around in a fancy car, talk about all your work accomplishments, and wear an expensive watch. I have a nice watch, too, but nobody ever bothers to ask me for money. You see, you brag about the things you've accomplished. Within a half hour of meeting you, I already know that the only way you think you can attract people is with your wealth. That's why you appeal to that certain personality, whereas a woman who's secure with herself doesn't want to hear that. It actually turns her off."

The Law of Attraction works with *everything*. Examine your life again and decide whether you're attracting the right people. If not, dig deep and find out why. How do you do that? By doing the exercises in this chapter, addressing the difficult questions I've asked, and figuring out all the things in your past that didn't satisfy you. What are your priorities? Are you generally positive or negative?

This universal law is one of the most powerful lessons you can learn. If you ever get frustrated with the individuals coming into your life, I want you to read this chapter over and over again. If you're surrounded by people who are wrong for you, I want you to figure out what's wrong with *you* right now. What are you not doing? What are you not embracing? Why are you not experiencing the beautiful life that you were meant to live?

The answers are already within you. You simply have to ask the right questions and honestly seek the truth. It takes guts, and it takes self-confidence. And I have no doubt that you can, and will, do it!

In the next chapter, we'll see how living in the past and blaming others for your problems can have a seriously negative impact on your ability to engage in enjoyable, long-term relationships.

■ ■ ■

CHAPTER 3

TAKE
RESPONSIBILITY

Have you even been on a first date and found yourself sitting across from someone whom you were really attracted to? Someone whom you were just amazed by? You may have even felt like you had a crush on this person because you found him or her so attractive—whether it was because of a certain style, a comment, or a vibe. You probably thought to yourself, *This is just going to be an amazing date.*

Imagine this: You go to the bathroom, come back, and there's someone new sitting at the table—someone quite different from the individual you found so attractive just a few minutes earlier. *What's different?* you may be wondering. Well, your date has launched into a monologue like you've never heard before. The second you returned from the bathroom, this person started telling you all about the past. Not only is your date rehashing old relationships, he or she is also detailing how wronged he or she was in every single one of them.

This person is complaining, and has turned into a *past-er.*

Now let me set something straight right at the beginning: I'm not talking about a *pastor.* I'm talking about past-ers: those who live in the *past.* These men and women constantly talk about all the awful things that happened to them five, ten, or more years ago. They just can't let go of what was and move on with their lives. And when you discover that your date is one of these people, you may soon realize that there's absolutely no future for the two of you.

Most past-ers are blamers—that is, they haven't taken full responsibility for anything they've done. They blame everyone who wronged them for everything bad that has ever occurred in their relationships. You've probably heard the term *poor me.* Well, these people definitely fall into the "poor me" category, but I personally prefer to call them past-ers.

These individuals come in all different variations. Some have been cheated on endlessly by their lovers and can't figure out why they always fall for those who betray them—it couldn't *possibly* have anything to do with them, right? They just seem to have bad luck when it comes to dating. Or do they?

Here's something for you to chew on: I believe that the vast majority of individuals who have been cheated on actually attracted the partners who betrayed them; in fact, they enable that behavior through their own negative energy. I'll just go ahead and say it: I'm convinced that those who complain about being cheated on are themselves 100 percent responsible for the cheating.

I know you're probably wondering, *What about those pathological cheaters who do it for the sheer enjoyment and thrill of it?* Sure, there are people like that. But, if you remember the Law of Attraction in dating from Chapter 2, you'll recall that you attract those who match the vibration you put out into the world. If you send out an energy that shows neediness and insecurity, you'll attract individuals who themselves are needy and insecure . . . and many cheaters possess these very issues. They're constantly requiring that their egos be stroked by a series of romantic partners who tell them they are handsome, beautiful, or the greatest lovers in the world.

You must look directly at yourself and learn how to take full responsibility for *all* of your actions. If you don't, you'll never move forward. Who are you attracting into your life, and why? Is it someone who's strong and self-confident, or is he or she weak and helpless?

■ ■ ■

A long time ago I learned a valuable lesson. Back in 1997, while living in Colorado, I was experiencing quite a bit of success in the car business. To be honest, I'd become quite greedy at this point in my life. I'd built a solid company and was making very good money, but I decided that I wanted to move to California, where I was planning to build an empire. In fact, one of my lifelong dreams was to live in Los Angeles. But instead, I moved to San Diego, a place I'd never previously considered calling home.

After making the move, I proceeded to get involved in a couple of different ventures. To make a long story short, one partner took advantage of me and stole my money. This put me in a downward spiral, and I went from bad to worse, financially speaking. Eventually, the whole thing just came crashing down on me. I ended up with maybe $20,000 in cash, and everything else was gone. My credit was destroyed, my businesses were gone, my life savings was decimated, and I was a complete mess.

I can remember sitting in my attorney's office after the shit had hit the fan. He looked at me and said, "We've got a couple of options. One, we can chase this guy down and try to recover some of the money. But that will cost *you* money, and we may very well never get a dime out of him. You've already tried and were unsuccessful, so you know that the funds have probably disappeared.

"Two, you can take the money you've got left and start all over again."

I looked at him and replied, "I'll never be able to move forward if I'm always looking into the past. So I don't want to look back—because if I go after him, which means thinking about this money and giving it energy, I'll never be able to make new money and embrace new opportunities. I'll take my $20,000, and I'll take my chances on my future in L.A."

And that's what I did.

A year later, when everything was running really well and I was back to making a healthy income, I ran into the guy who ripped me off. At this point, I was feeling good about myself—full of energy and confidence. But when I looked at him, I could plainly see that he'd become old, tired, and haggard. The negative things he'd done to me, and likely to others, were running him down. While I had moved on and was putting my energy into the present and future, this guy was stuck in the past—chained down by all his guilt.

Here's another example. I once lent some money to a close friend, who proceeded to never pay me back. I was angry with him for a few years, which in turn kept me from attracting the money to pay *myself* back. Instead of letting go of the situation, I was mired in it, and I couldn't get on with my life. That all changed when this friend called and asked me to tell him: "I love you, and I forgive you for what you did to me." As soon as I did that, it was like a dark cloud lifted from over my head. In that moment, I finally realized that our friendship was more important than the debt, and I decided to let go of the anger I felt toward him. I was even able to attract the money to repay myself for the financial hole I'd created.

You can use this example in every aspect of your life, especially dating. Every time you look backward, you're angry, or you're frustrated about an ex—whether you talk about him or her on a date with another person, or are someone who jumps into past-er mode—you're simply putting negative energy out into the universe. You waste your time focused on the people who have wronged you, cheated on you, not called you back, broken your heart, taken money from you, or whatever it may be.

Who cares? Your date certainly doesn't. And you shouldn't either.

The longer you exhaust your energy complaining about all the people who have hurt you, the longer you will be stuck there and not processing the path to move forward. Don't get me wrong—your past is *wonderful*. It's where you learned all your lessons about life, and it's been absolutely vital to your becoming the most powerful version of yourself. That's the positive side.

However, too many of us get so stuck there that we're unable to unlock the energy that's within each one of us and become free again.

If you're obsessed with all the men or women who have ever compromised your trust in past relationships, I can guarantee that right now you're having a hard time initiating new romances, because you haven't processed certain issues. All of your relationships offer lessons to learn, whether they're with the person who ripped you off or broke your heart. Each one had energy that you welcomed into your life.

As I've already mentioned, if you've been cheated on over and over again, then you're attracting that situation to yourself—either because you haven't processed your past or accepted responsibility for it. Blamers and finger-pointers remain stuck, it's that simple. They're always looking at their past with anger and disappointment; and they don't realize that they can't control, reshape, or correct what's already happened.

The only thing you do have control of is the present. Only when you have forgiven (and embraced) all the people who have done you wrong, and learned the necessary lessons from those situations, can you be living 100 percent in this moment. This is when the partners you've been dreaming about will begin to enter your life.

Ask yourself, *What did I do to influence someone else?* Each action has a cause and an effect, and past-ers are usually pattern repeaters.

If you've been betrayed, it's likely that you've played a role in creating that situation. That is, if you were cheated on in the past, you may decide—perhaps subconsciously—that the minute anything goes wrong in your relationship, you will defend against being hurt again by holding back emotionally from your new love interest. And if you remain closed from this person, he or she may decide to venture elsewhere.

People are unfaithful for a variety of reasons. Some behave in this way because they find it fun or exciting or dangerous—that's just how they're wired. Others cheat because they lack the intimacy they once had in a previous relationship, or simply as a reaction to something their partners have done.

It's important to understand that there's a cause and effect in everything in life—even cheating. If you've been let down, take a close look at those relationships and ask yourself, *How might I have caused this person to stray?* Were you emotionally unavailable? Was there a lack of intimacy due to fear? Were there unaddressed sexual issues? Identifying the role you may have played in your partner's cheating is critically important because I truly believe that when you stop holding back, you will never be cheated on again.

■ ■ ■

Here's an exercise to help work through issues from the past that are stifling you. Create lists of everything in your romances that made you feel good, hurt, pissed off, angry, and loved. I believe that this activity is absolutely necessary in order for you to examine and become accountable for everything you did in these past relationships.

Have you ever been in a relationship that felt as if it were a competition? If I scratch your back, then you scratch mine. Or if you *don't* scratch my back, I'm not going to scratch yours. This is a situation where ego is driving everything; communication isn't safe; and neither one of you is letting go, compromising, or even acknowledging what's going wrong and working on it.

In order to let go, trust your partner, and really move forward, you need to love this person the way he or she needs to be loved. Because when you do so, you're also loving yourself. When you get to this point, you'll be acting selflessly, not expecting anything in return, and receiving what you need because you will have dropped the ego and processed your unresolved relationship issues.

Take a look at your list. You don't want to be that person who is constantly blaming other people for your past relationships and failures. Nothing, as you know from the beginning of this chapter, will ever turn any-body off more on a date than talking negatively about an ex. Take full responsibility for everything you've done in your past, embrace it, and learn from it.

Everything.

When you're able to move on with your life, you're going to be 100 percent present and available. You're not going to get angry because someone reminds you of the guy or gal who once cheated on you. Your entire future is going to seem new, different, and exciting; and you won't experience the same frustrating results over and over again.

Look at your life. Look at your list. Accept and em-brace what you did right and what you did wrong. Ex-amine your past relationships—how many of them were repeats of older ones?

It took me until I was well into my 20s before I was able to learn these lessons. It was as if every woman I went out with was the same—each one just looked a lit-tle bit different. When you can get on with life, it means that you've accepted yourself. You've taken responsibil-ity for every choice you've made, and you've forgiven anybody who's ever wronged you. Doing so will allow you to finally go out and find an intense, amazing, in-credible, passionate, loving relationship that satisfies you on every level.

■ ■ ■

Far too many people allow excuses to dictate their lives. In the next chapter, we'll take a close look at ex-cuses and how the failure to take responsibility for your shortcomings—and thus taking the steps to ad-dress them—can prevent you from finding the love of your life.

■ ■ ■

CHAPTER 4

WHAT'S YOUR EXCUSE?

When I first started teaching seminars years ago, I put together a website called What's Your Excuse? (Some of you who have been following me for a long time probably remember it.) Its focus was to address the excuses we all make for not doing things and finding ways to get around them. Similarly, this chapter is all about the excuses we make that get in our way.

But before I begin on this topic, though, I want to talk about the mind-set that inhabits people who live an excuse-filled life. It's called *catastrophe mode*. When you're in this mode, you have an "oh no" mentality. "Oh no, things are going to go wrong!" "Oh no, they don't like me!" "Oh no!"

I know how this is, because I've been there. Let me share a story with you. Back when I was living in New York City a long, long time ago, I was working as a bartender. One of my steady clients would not engage people socially at all. He would just sit there at the bar, drink his beers, and leave. He always tipped well, was very courteous, and was just generally a nice man. But one day my curiosity got the best of me.

"You seem like a good guy, but never talk to anybody. Why not?"

He answered, "I just don't feel it, to be honest with you. I'm in my head a lot, which to me is like being in a really bad part of town. When I try to go out socially, it's as if I go to the worst place in the city. Imagine being in the most dangerous neighborhood in the middle of the night, and you're all alone with a pocketful of money."

I started laughing and said, "I would feel really paranoid."

He continued, "That's how I feel all the time. I'm fine at work, since that's the good neighborhood—it's like Beverly Hills. I'm very successful in the office. But when I come out at night, I feel like I'm running for my life. I'm in my head. I'm in my excuses. And I'm in my fears."

A lot of people are like this—they'll go out on Friday and Saturday night, sit at the bar, have a drink, not have the guts to talk to anyone, and wonder why they're not meeting people. They're living the definition of insanity: doing the same thing over and over again and expecting a different result.

These individuals are not socially inept and don't have problems communicating. They just have an extreme fear of the opposite sex, which they don't know how to overcome. It's common for these men and women to put themselves in social situations over and over again, hoping something will change. Even though they're in the slums of their minds, constantly getting "beat up" by the opposite sex, they still go out every night, hoping that they'll stumble across somebody who will notice and like them.

This is the kind of client that I have to rebuild from the ground up. We start by practicing how to say hello, smile, and observe others. We do everything we can to get them to realize that *people* aren't scary—it's just their *thoughts* that are scary. Their fears and excuses protect them from ever trying something different. What's the worst that can happen if they were to try a new approach? They might actually succeed.

Because so many of us are so quick to rely on excuses, we allow fear to dictate us. I know what it's like to live this way, inside my head—I've been there and done that. However, when I find myself doing so now, I immediately exit that bad neighborhood and head back to the Beverly Hills of my mind.

The reason you don't talk to someone in the gym is because you're going to have to find a new place to work out if she's not interested in you. Or you don't approach someone while you're in line to pay for your groceries because you're going to have to find a new store if he doesn't ask you out.

It comes down to your mind-set and belief system. You have the choice whether or not you're going to believe your false justifications and allow them to overtake you, but, unfortunately, I see people live excuse-filled lives all the time. They say things like, "There's nobody worth meeting in this city" or "There are no good men my age—they all want to date younger women." I've heard every excuse in the book, so I don't really care what yours is. To tell you the truth, they're all just made-up stories that prevent you from going out and finding true love.

We can all come up with explanations for why we don't do things, why we're not as successful as we'd like to be, why we don't meet people, and why our relationships never work out. We can create as many cop-outs as we want and use them all day long: "I just can't seem to get personal with people," or "I have trouble listening." If I began listing them, I could probably go on forever . . . but the bottom line is I'm not going to. This entire book is designed so we *don't* buy into this way of thinking.

■ ■ ■

It's easy to allow your excuses to dictate what you do, because your comfort zone is your excuse. "I'm not going to go over there to talk to girl, because, you know what? If I start a conversation with her in front of her three friends, they're all going to be talking about me."

I'm going to mention this again and again throughout the book: People are consumed by their own problems and issues—all they care about is their own crap. If you could take a peek inside their heads, I'm sure you would find that they're in a bad, bad neighborhood. So when it comes to your excuses, they're just protective barriers to keep you in the state of mind that you're choosing to be in. I know that firsthand because I've done it before, and recently I've been doing so again.

My back isn't in great shape. I blew out the disc between L4 and L5 in my spine, and as a result I go into catastrophe mode whenever I feel a pain in my back, no matter how big or how small. All I can think is *Oh, no. Here we go again.*

So, what happens when I jump into catastrophe mode? My back will go out every time. In fact, I was in Boston for a short visit while writing this book. As I stepped out of a cab, I put all my pressure on one leg, and my back went into spasms. I immediately thought, *Why does this always have to happen when I travel? Here we go again!* Even though I'd been feeling pretty good and doing a lot of rehab—something called the Egoscue Method, which I believe is fantastic—I reverted to desperation and fear.

Can you see the problem with this mind-set? Traveling is my passion, similar to how your passion might be meeting people or cooking elaborate dinners. So just as I was worried about messing up my back while doing what I love, when your friend calls to go out on a Friday night, you might be thinking, *Oh no. Whenever I go to that bar, I never seem to be able to talk to anyone.*

When I got out of the cab, my back hurt, I couldn't breathe, and I went down to the ground. But I told myself, *I'm going to stand up, and hopefully I'll be okay.* I did get right back on my feet, and I turned out to be fine. I realized at that moment that all the hard work I was doing in Egoscue was not only working on my muscles, it was reformulating my thoughts as well. I understood that my back wasn't going to break or go out just because I tweaked it. I knew my body was strong enough and that I was going to be okay.

And I spent the rest of the weekend enjoying myself. I even felt fine on the entire flight back to California. I survived. Just like you're going to survive when you go to a party and stand there in an oh-no moment. Even though you'll say you don't know what to do, in reality you *do.* After all, you're reading this book, and you know how to talk.

The mind is incredibly powerful, and every one of us has the capability to blast through the excuses that get in our way. I know this because I have personally conquered my own oh-no moments. I'm healing myself, and I'm learning how powerful the mind is. You see, I want to stay in the Beverly Hills of my mind. I don't want to go into the deep, dark alleys.

Here's one of the best exercises in the entire world: Write down every excuse you can come up with for why you can't talk to the individuals you typically see during your day, from the gym to the supermarket to parties. Be sure to include all the places where you see people you're attracted to. Now, as you read through your list of excuses, realize that *every single one of them is BS.*

"I'm not pretty enough." Yes, you are. Go to Walmart. Go to Target. Go to Costco. If you walk around for a while and look at people who are similar to you, you'll soon see that many of them are in relationships— they've got rings on their fingers or they're strolling the aisles with their significant others.

"I'm not tall enough." I hear that from guys all the time. Notice the men around you. They're not all with dates who are shorter than they are—many women prefer shorter men.

"I'm in the wrong age range. I've missed my opportunity." Really? No matter how old you are, there are tons of relationships involving people who are your age.

I've heard all these excuses over and over again, ad nauseam. So I want you to analyze them, see others in the same situation, and realize that your reasoning has kept you from having the social life you've always wanted. In reality, you possess all the power you need to stop hiding behind your justifications. You have the ability to get out of Oh-no-ville and Catastrophe-ville and into a positive, abundant life.

■ ■ ■

I once had a client who was an overweight man in his 30s. At the end of our first day together, he told me, "I'm so excited to be working with you because I'll be able to use all this information you've given me in seven months."

"What? Why seven months? How did you come up with that number?" I asked.

He responded, "That's when I'm going to be my ideal weight. Between now and then, I'm going to try a bunch of different diets, and I'm sure that one of them will work. I picked out seven, and each of them is going to take a month to complete. So at the end of the month, I'll know which diet is working and stick with it."

Now that was an approach I'd never heard before. I told him, "That's ridiculous. Maybe you're at your ideal weight right now. Maybe you're supposed to be this way."

"No, no, no," he replied. "I've got to be fit, I've got to be trim. Women don't want a body like mine."

So I asked my client to take off his shirt. Soon he was standing there with his shirt in his hands, trying to cover up his body. I looked at him and I said, "You look *great*. This is *your* body. Love it, nurture it, and embrace it every single day. And get your butt to the gym! Here are the exercises you need to do: swim for 20 minutes and lift weights for 30 minutes a day. Now let's go pick out some food you can eat." And that's what we did. Of course, as we were grocery shopping, we were also meeting women. What I finally taught him was that he might very well have been seven months from having the perfect body, but it was still just his excuse.

In reality, you meet new people every single day. No one's looking at you and thinking, *Wow—I'm going to be really attracted to this person in seven months*. It's all about having the right attitude—believing in yourself. You will *never* have the perfect body, so stop trying to reach that goal. If you want to truly look your best, then commit to going on a diet and working out.

And in the meantime, introduce yourself and smile when you meet someone new, because once you start working out, you'll feel much better. And the better you feel, the more approachable you're going to be, which will open a lot of doors for you along the way. In fact, someone is probably looking at you right now, thinking that you already have the perfect body.

■ ■ ■

In the next chapter, we'll consider whether or not you are the kind of person you would be attracted to. If you are, you can be sure that *others* will be as well.

■ ■ ■

CHAPTER 5

WOULD YOU DATE YOURSELF?

I want you to be completely honest when you answer this question: Would you date yourself?

Think about it—are you fun to be around? Are you someone who's at ease having conversations? Do you pick out cool things to do on dates? Are you romantic? Do people enjoy themselves when they're around you? Are you interesting? Do you have a lot to talk about—and when you do, are you passionate about what you're saying? Do you speak with authority? Are you someone who is well-rounded and can easily participate in discussions? Do you listen carefully to others and learn from what they have to say? Are you a healthy person, both physically and emotionally? Are you somebody who takes the good with the bad and can keep things on an even keel? Are you a drama queen or king? Are you insecure and nervous? Are you constantly annoyed at everyone because you feel that the world owes you?

Whatever you are, would you want to date *you?*

■ ■ ■

My client Marco reveled in a poor-me attitude. He was the kind of person who just couldn't look beyond all the wrongs that had been inflicted on him in past relationships. He was the king of first dates—he had lots of them, but he could never get a second one with the same woman, and he couldn't figure out why this kept happening. That is, until he hired me. It took a while, but I eventually got Marco to realize that *he* was the reason that girls wouldn't go out with him again. The problem wasn't with his prospective mates—it was mostly with *him.*

During our time together, I helped him realize that on every date he was always bashing an ex, talking negatively about his love life, and expressing how unhappy he was at his job. In addition, whenever the conversation turned to a topic he didn't know much about or felt like he couldn't participate in, he always tried to change the subject—giving his date the impression that he wasn't even listening.

So what did I do next? I actually went out on a date with him. I sat at a table next to Marco and his new love interest, and I listened to the way he conducted himself. I immediately realized that he was swinging for the fences with a *very* needy poor-poor-pitiful-me act.

After identifying the problem, we worked together to try to fix it. I explained to Marco that the whole world doesn't owe him; and that he had to start believing in himself, forgiving the people who had wronged him, and taking full responsibility for his life. Finally, I told him that if he didn't love himself, he was never going to find the healthy, incredible, truthful relationship he so badly wanted.

■ ■ ■

When I ask you the question "Would you date yourself?" I'm really telling you that you have to become the kind of person you would like to meet, date, and spend the rest of your life with. You can't be someone who just sits on the couch and watches TV every single night. You've got to go out, be a part of something, and always be learning. You have to embrace life. There is a new and exciting you inside who's just aching to come out.

You have to do things that expand your horizons and help you see the wonderful world around you. You have to experience new things that will make you more interesting to be with. In other words, you're not going to meet an exciting stranger at the grocery store and immediately bring him or her home with you . . . that is a recipe for disaster (and danger).

I have personally found that the easiest and most powerful way to do this is to think of one new thing to learn each week. So, for example, go to an art gallery this week. And while you're there, ask questions. Look at people, engage them in conversations, and find out how the paintings make them feel.

What's so fantastic about trying new things is that during the course of becoming a well-balanced, fun, exciting person, you're also meeting a lot of new individuals whom you may share many interests with. As you're getting out there, becoming someone who can contribute intelligent insights in social situations, you're interacting with those who are probably either doing the same thing or just enjoying their own passions. Either way, you're broadening your horizons.

Many people spend a lot of awkward moments wondering what to say, but the thing is, by forcing yourself to have experiences outside of your comfort zone, you're able to relate to people on many different levels. So you'll never, ever be lacking for words when you're introduced to someone you had your eye one, because you'll always be ready to strike up a conversation. And those who always have something to talk about are the best dates, since they're usually the best listeners—which in turn allows them to share what they've learned.

I want you to get out there and involve yourself in activities that are outside of your comfort zone—ones you would never normally do. But be sure to choose things that interest or intrigue you. Maybe learn about wine or coffee, or take a cooking class. You can go to a new film one week, or a special event or grand opening the next. Believe me, you'll actually start to enjoy your life more by doing this.

It could even be as simple as sitting by yourself at the bar of a new restaurant and talking to people around you. The more you experience, the more you can share, and the more datable you become.

When I was single, I was always meeting tons of women at the local Whole Foods Market. Whole Foods was such a great place for me—it was my home turf. I was passionate about quality food and being healthy, so it was easy to communicate with people because I sampled a lot of the products and knew which ones were good and which ones weren't. The conversations were easy, simple, and natural; and I always had something to add because I was well-rounded in staying in shape and eating right.

Again, the more you do, the more you have to talk about. If you're somebody who sits at home on the sofa and plays video games or watches TV all the time, when you're out to dinner, you have nothing to contribute—nothing at all. But by doing this exercise, guess what happens? You make more acquaintances, expand your network, get invited to parties, and, as a result, get more dates.

■ ■ ■

Tony, a really great guy and a client of mine came to me one time and said, "David, I don't know what to talk about on a date at all."

"Talk about how your day went today, or what you've been doing this week," I answered.

Tony looked at me and asked, "Why would anyone want to hear about that? I'm not interesting at work, it's just boring numbers. At night I go home and make myself the same dinner every night I love my spaghetti and meatballs. And I watch the same shows every week. So when I go on a date, what am I going to talk about?"

"We have a problem," I admitted. "You just shot down your entire date right there. You have nothing interesting to say, because your life is a routine. What have you done in the last year? Have you gone on any vacations?"

"No, I don't take any trips. I've just been working, and I've been doing that for years," Tony replied.

"What do you do on the weekends?"

"I do errands—that's it."

I pushed further. "Do you talk to people when you do these things? Do you strike up conversations? Do you make an effort to learn about new things—something besides spaghetti and meatballs?"

"No, I just run my errands. I don't even see people. I just get the things that I need—the pasta, the meat, the sauce, my dry cleaning—and go home."

"Do you know what your big problem is?" I asked. "You don't experience life. When I go shopping, I talk about the food, I chitchat, I pick up something interesting and make a comment about it. When I run my errands—even just picking up my dry cleaning—I engage people and find out something new. When I go to lunch, I don't eat the same thing every day. If I see someone who's eating a dish that looks really good, I'll ask him or her a question about it. And every day that goes by, I learn more and more, which gives me countless opportunities to pass things on to others."

I recommended that my client go back to drawing board, since the way he was living, he had nothing to offer anyone. I attempted to have him think of *anything* he wanted to do outside of his regular routine—for example, trips, cooking classes, concerts, or plays. To start with, I told him that he should buy some travel and cooking magazines—and then read them instead of watching TV one night.

■ ■ ■

If you want to be successful at dating, you've got to become curious about the world around you so that you become a more well-rounded person. And a great exercise to accomplish this goal is to date yourself.

Pick a day sometime this week to take yourself out. Walk around your city and do some activities that you've always wanted to do but have never gotten around to. Everywhere you go, talk to people you meet and share your experiences with them. If you're standing in line at Starbucks, ask the person in front of you what his favorite coffee is and why. If you go to an art museum, ask that cute girl who her favorite artist is and why. Just get lost in your own curiosity, and share your adventures with others as you go through them.

Make time every day to become more aware of the world around you. Glance at the home page of **Yahoo .com** or turn on CNN and watch for 15 minutes so you know what's going on in the news. When you do these simple things as part of your normal routine, you'll be able to contribute to conversations. And when you're able to do so, you'll have an opportunity to confidently engage people, possibly opening the door to an entirely new group of the dating pool. You'll soon find somebody amazing to be with and enjoy your life so much more.

In reality, you'll be more open, more real, and a more exciting person to date. Why? Because you're going to know yourself better and have an accurate picture of who you want to be.

Not only will you discover all this by dating yourself, but you'll begin to embrace your truth. You'll also no longer be so negative, because you'll be able to forgive all the people in your life who have done you wrong— all of them. You'll take full responsibility for everyone you've been with. By dating yourself, I guarantee that you'll start learning how to love yourself and enjoying your life more fully.

And that is extremely powerful medicine indeed.

■ ■ ■

In the next chapter, we'll explore how rejection is actually something entirely different from how you may currently think of it.

■ ■ ■

CHAPTER 6

THERE'S NO SUCH THING AS REJECTION

It's interesting to me how people will start doing all the right things to meet their perfect match after hearing what I have to say about how they can get in touch with their truth. They do the exercises that I've described in this book. They go out of their way to start talking to others; making acquaintances; and becoming more vulnerable, open, and real. And they begin to practice abundance, because they come to realize that they can meet people anytime, anywhere.

If there's one absolute truth I can impart upon you, it's that there's no shortage of interesting men and women to date in this world. There are so many potential mates out there who want to meet, be with, and experience *you*. And once you realize that, you can make an unlimited number of connections.

But guess what? Not every single eligible bachelor or bachelorette in the world is going to be a good match, and not everyone you date is going to want to go out a second time. Sorry, but that's the truth. And even though you may think that your love interest is the living, breathing personification of everything you've ever dreamed of, he or she may not agree. And when that same level of love and affection isn't returned with the same intensity, you're bound to take it to heart.

■ ■ ■

Let's say you go on a first date with someone who's straight out of your fantasy. You have a great time, and you're certain that everything went as well as it possibly could have. So you call the person the next day to gush about what a wonderful time you had, but he or she doesn't answer the phone . . . and doesn't call you back. You may very well decide to take this apparent rejection quite personally. Immediately, you doubt yourself—even though up until now, you were self-confident and sure of yourself. Instead, you stop embracing the powerful, amazing, sexy, and beautiful individual you are and fall apart at the seams.

As the days pass and you *still* don't hear from your date, you start to go crazy. You bring in your friends and regurgitate and reenact every moment of that special night—getting into circular conversations with no end in sight. You mention the same things to the same people over and over again, hoping that they can figure out what went wrong. And all of the self-assuredness you had just a few days ago is now being stripped away. It's as if you've been given your kryptonite. And your kryptonite has you on the ropes.

A week has now passed, and by this point you're ob-sessing about your dream date who left you high and dry. You want to forget it and go out and have a good time, but you can't concentrate or focus on anyone else because you are completely consumed by this one in-dividual who decided—*after only one date*—never to call back.

So, while all of this is going on, you miss countless opportunities to attract and meet somebody spectacu-lar. The pity party that you've thrown for yourself repels new people from wanting to meet you—it's like a force field that keeps everyone at a distance. All the insecuri-ties have returned, and you're manifesting a new disease called rejection.

In reality, rejection is just an insecurity in your own mind. If you think about it, you realize there's actually no such thing—it doesn't exist. It's a made-up thought, a made-up word.

If a potential partner chooses not to call you back, it's not that you've suddenly stopped being the amazing person you've always been. That's not the case at all. The truth is that you created this new disease for yourself. You're the one who looks in the mirror each morning and decides what your attitude is going to be for the day. In fact, I can guarantee that whoever you're obsessing about isn't sitting at home poking pins into a voodoo doll with a photo of your face taped to it, thinking about how much he or she enjoyed hurting you. It's *you* who is wallowing in this depressed state—*alone*.

How do you even truly get to know someone after just one date? In reality, you have an illusion in your mind of who you believe he or she is. And instead of thinking, *You know, I've done this to other people myself. I've gone out on some great dates, but then I woke up in the morning and didn't want to take the relationship any further.*

Instead of realizing that it's not a big deal—that even you have dropped the ball when a potential partner wasn't the right match for you—you insist that it's all about *you,* and right now you're nothing more than a big loser.

But wait! It's not the end of the world. It's actually a blessing that this person had the conviction to break things off when it was clear that you were the only one who was excited about a relationship. You've been given a new beginning.

So that's what I mean when I say that there's no such thing as rejection. Embracing this positive attitude when you hit a momentary speed bump in your dating life gives you an opportunity to go out and meet other fantastic people who are going to be totally jazzed about being with you.

When something in your love life doesn't happen, you've got to get out of rejection mode right away. There's absolutely nothing to be gained by getting stuck in that place for any period of time. Unfortunately, I've had many clients who—after being ignored by someone they really wanted to go out with—end up depressed for four, five, or even six months or more. These people get desperate about themselves and either push away the next dating opportunity or settle for someone they don't want, desire, or deserve. They get involved in a relationship based on being Mr. or Ms. Needy.

Finding the love of your life takes time—it's hard work. Is it fun? Yes. Enjoyable? Yes. But hard work nonetheless. You can't give up before you've given it everything you've got. There's no reason for you to become a victim of self-doubt and fear. Every day you must wake up and realize that people are not out there to hurt, deceive, or reject you. Life is a series of choices, and for whatever reason, that girl or guy from Saturday night chose not to pursue a relationship with you. It doesn't mean that you're not a fantastic, sexy, incredible, gorgeous person. All it means is that you two weren't a match. Suck it up, and move on.

■ ■ ■

When I was 24 years old I met this beautiful girl. We went out, and like most of us do when we go out on dates, I thought we had great chemistry. (In reality, we don't really know how to read or interpret our own dates. That's why we tend to go straight to our friends afterward and ask them to analyze what the other person said or did—we rely on the opinions of people who weren't there and don't know anything about how things went.) Anyway, I remember meeting this woman and thinking to myself, *I really like her.* I wanted to do something really cool to really make an impression, so I scraped together a couple of bucks—I was really young at the time, and a couple of bucks was a lot for me!—and bought a bottle of wine and a little card. And on the card I wrote: "Name where you'd like to share this great bottle of wine. Call me. David," and included my phone number.

I knew where she worked, so I stood in front of her office building and waited until a kid came along. I said, "Hey buddy, can you do me a favor? Take this up to the 11th floor and bring it to a girl named Lisa." And he did.

So there I was, standing in front of this building on a bitterly cold winter day in New York City with my jacket wide open. (I always had my jacket open in the middle of winter because I wanted to look cool, even when it was freezing cold outside.) And then I started to daydream about the new love of my life. I imagined us having a picnic in Central Park—the sun was shining and the air was warm. We were sharing a bottle of wine and gazing into each other's eyes. She was telling me how much she loved me and how she couldn't think of anyone but me. At one point I think I even imagined us moving in together—wearing matching sweatshirts and settling into an eternal state of domestic tranquility.

The kid came down a few minutes later, waking me from my trance. He looked at me and said, "Aww, man! She's really hot!"

"Yeah, I know." I then asked him what Lisa had done when he gave her the bottle, and he said she'd just smiled and taken it.

Perfect.

So then I did what anyone would do in the days before cell phones, text messages, and e-mail—I went home, sat by my phone, and waited for it to ring. And I waited and waited, and I waited some more, but it didn't ring. I went out to dinner, and every 15 minutes I left my table, put a quarter in the phone booth, punched in my magic answering-machine code, and heard the recorded voice say, "No new messages." I got home after dinner: no phone call. I got up the next day: no phone call.

The phone never rang, and Lisa never called. I felt rejected, and I wondered where I'd made a mistake. I must have done *something* wrong—maybe I bought her the wrong bottle of wine, or maybe I didn't write a good message. I beat myself up as thoroughly as I possibly could. I got deep inside my head, and I created a boxing match starring me versus myself. I put on the gloves, and I knocked myself into a pulp. In fact, I spent an entire week battering myself. I was disappointed, and I no longer had any self-confidence.

Think about that: I only went out with this girl once, sent her a bottle of wine, and asked her to call me . . . and she didn't respond. I decided the chemistry actually wasn't there between us, and I took it as rejection.

So I hope you'll embrace the lesson that I had to learn the hard way: rejection is all in your head. My failed relationship with Lisa didn't mean that I wasn't a good person, or that the wine gesture wouldn't work with another woman. In fact, I've done it—with more successful results—many times since then. A lot of people will do something one time, get turned down, and never do it again. That's a mistake.

And a couple months later, I met a woman whom I ended up having a great relationship with, which allowed me to quickly forget all about how I felt when Lisa didn't call.

■ ■ ■

A man named Bill came to one of my boot camps (which, you should know, require that participants must be ready to voice all of their fears and excuses) and told me, "I understand that the entire week I'll be approaching women, talking to them, and becoming more of a natural around them. But I've got to tell you something—I don't know if I can do this. I don't think I can handle being rejected. At the gym I used to go to, I finally got the nerve to talk to a woman on the treadmill next to me who I'd been staring at for months. When I finally decided to say something, she didn't even take off her headphones—she totally ignored me. I ended up having to join a new gym in another neighborhood because I was too embarrassed to see her again."

I said, "Maybe she didn't hear you. Maybe her music was too loud."

Bill responded, "Yeah, I never thought of that. But it doesn't matter—women reject me all the time. I look at them and they look the other way. I'm just an ugly guy."

I stared at him and shot right back, "You're not ugly. You're actually a pretty decent-looking guy. You allowed one experience to ruin your entire mind-set. Rejection really is all in our minds, and it means nothing. She didn't turn you down, and she didn't say she wasn't interested in you. She probably didn't even know you were talking to her. And this definitely doesn't mean you're ugly."

The lesson for Bill, and all of us, is that chemistry between people is a two-way street. We have to be attractive to someone, and he or she has to be attractive to us. We must learn to embrace this concept.

Let's talk about an exercise you can do right now to help you get past this rejection thing that's keeping you from meeting and dating your perfect match.

Consider a time when you were obsessed with a potential mate, reached out to him or her, and got no response in return. It can also be a person you started to like a little—or a lot—and then the fling suddenly ended. I don't mean someone you went out with for a few months and then broke up; I'm talking about a maximum of only two or three dates.

Now reflect on all the times in your life that you've felt rejected in these extremely short relationships, and try to remember for how long you suffered afterward. A day? A week? A month? A year? Write down the length of time for each instance.

Next, total up all the hours you spent in this "rejection zone," and record that number at the bottom of your list. How much of your life have you wasted away, feeling miserable that you were rejected after hanging out with someone just a few times? I did this exercise with a client of mine, and she came to the realization that she'd wasted *two and a half years* of her life being obsessed and tortured (at least in her mind) by people she barely knew. That's two and a half years too long.

Instead of remaining in a rejection zone, live your dating life in an abundant way, and make the following

mantra a part of your daily life (simply change the gen-
der if necessary):

> I'm an unbelievable, incredible, fantastic
> person. If a man [woman] chooses not to be with
> me, then that's *his* [*her*] choice. If I go out on
> a date and it doesn't work out because the guy
> [girl] doesn't call me, that's fine. I'm not going to
> get hung up on *anybody.* If I like a man [woman]
> and he [she] doesn't reciprocate by responding
> within 72 hours, I'm going love myself by going
> out the very next day and meeting other men
> [women].

The longer you remain stuck, the harder it's going
to be to recover. For example, if you're naturally very
shy, and you've worked really hard to build up the confidence to ask someone out, you're more likely to stay in
the rejection zone longer and revert to your old habits.
So maintain your determination and sense of adventure
by getting back out there right away. Give the other person 72 hours to get back to you, and if you don't hear
anything, it's time to move on.

Here's another exercise that will help you better understand your relationships. For every girl- or boyfriend
you've had, write down how quickly the person called
you back after the first date and how many weeks it took
until you knew you were a couple. In the same way as
you did in the previous exercise, I want you to tally the
numbers. Now, compare this amount of time to how
long you wasted feeling sorry for yourself.

■ ■ ■

Every great relationship starts with one thing, and
that one thing is called *momentum.* Here's how it usually

works: You go out with somebody who you think is absolutely great. You follow up soon after, he or she gets back to you right away, and suddenly things are hot and heavy. We've all been there and experienced it—the connection and passion is very real (this will be addressed in much more detail in the next chapter).

I'll share a story with you about a client of mine named Rob. One of my favorite exercises is to have a vacation day, where I have people pick a neighborhood in their city that they never go to and spend the whole day exploring. And that's exactly what I told him to do.

Rob is generally a pretty shy guy, and he really wanted to work on his skills of meeting women naturally. The goal was that he would ultimately feel comfortable enough to strike up a conversation with someone he found attractive, whether he was in the elevator at work or at his favorite haunts.

So he followed my advice, and one day he went to the other side of Chicago from where he lives. His job was to be a tourist in his own city from noon until midnight. For him, this was like going to the moon. He went to stores he'd never been in, saw things he'd never seen, and encountered many new people. And he was as inquisitive as a child—asking questions, listening, and learning all about the area—just like a tourist on vacation.

Eight o'clock arrived, and Rob decided to check out a jazz bar that some women had told him was a lot of fun. He walked in and, lo and behold, there was a beautiful lady working the coat check. As he handed her his jacket, he casually struck up a conversation. But then the music began and the lights went down, so he had to be quiet.

But Rob didn't want things to end there—he wanted to keep talking to her! So he thought, *What would David do in this situation? He certainly wouldn't let this opportunity pass.* Then he looked at the woman and asked, "Do you have a pen and something to write with?" When she handed him a pad and a pen, he scribbled a few words on a page and handed it to her, just like he would have in the fourth grade. He gave it to her, she read it immediately . . . and they continued to write notes back and forth during the entire performance.

Finally, two hours later, after the music had finished, my client looked at the woman, and they both burst into laughter. Then he passed her one more note: "What's your phone number so we can get together?"

I don't know how long they lasted—because Rob was happy and satisfied and didn't need my help any longer. But however things turned out, he learned the power of communication and stepping out of his comfort zone. Think about how *you* do that when you're on vacation. Now it's your turn to take a trip across town and spend the day being a tourist.

■ ■ ■

Even if you don't have much dating experience, I'm sure you've had at least a little. You know what feels right—when a relationship is real and everything just clicks—and what doesn't. So why would you want to force something that's not working or isn't meant to be? Why would you want to call a person over and over again, desperately thinking, *God, if I can just get her [him] on the phone one more time, I know I can get her [him] to go out with me again!* Or why would you want to hash and rehash your love issues with all your friends and relatives, until people start avoiding your calls?

Why do you sell yourself short?

Wake up—you're not on sale! You're not marked down at a department store. So starting today—*right now*—I want you to move forward with your life and promise yourself that you're not going to waste any more time worrying about rejection, because these are precious hours that you'll never get back. Instead, you could be out there meeting people.

Make your call, give the other person three days to respond, and then proceed with pride. There's no such thing as rejection! It's a made up emotion, and your mind is extremely powerful—it can create any world you want. It's up to you to decide that you no longer want to feel hurt, regardless of the outcome.

You've got the ability. Now it's time to use it.

You know how it is when you've been sick for a few days, and you get tired of letting it rule your life. You say to yourself, *Come on. I'm going to wake up tomorrow and feel better.* And you know what, many times that's exactly what ends up happening. This works because your mind really does have that much influence. It can also help you conquer rejection with the positive thoughts that I've given you in this chapter.

You're a beautiful, sexy, amazing, confident person. So if someone doesn't want to be with you, that's his or her choice. Stop acting like a complete and utter baby when this happens. After all, that's what dating is all about.

And the quicker you get over it, the quicker you'll be back on the road to finding that most incredible, loving, fantastic relationship you deserve.

■ ■ ■

Commitment, desire, and discipline are all essential elements to finding success in dating. In the next chapter, we'll explore why, as well as how you can use this knowledge to your benefit.

■ ■ ■

CHAPTER 7

CDD: COMMITMENT, DESIRE, AND DISCIPLINE

I was coaching a client during a weekend-long session one time, and things happened to be going really well. It was fantastic in every way, as we worked really hard and broke through a lot of fears and barriers. Most important, we had identified the proper mind-set for successfully dating women.

By the end of our time together, this guy had introduced himself to a lot of people and experienced things that he never had before. Throughout his life, he'd lacked confidence due to being inside his head and doubting himself when it came to meeting the opposite sex. And let me give you a little more background: This was a very successful man in every other area of his life.

If you saw him, you'd never think that he could suffer from "approach anxiety" or any of the other self-created issues that were going on in his mind.

So as things were coming to a close, he looked at me and said, "This is the best weekend I've ever had, and I thank you for coaching me. There's only one more thing you can leave me with: how do I make sure all of this sticks?"

"That's easy," I replied. "Discipline. Without discipline, nothing will work."

"Could you go a little deeper?" he asked. "What does discipline have to do with this?"

"Everything we did this weekend proved that you were capable of being a powerful, strong, confident guy—someone who can walk around and talk to women naturally, without using pick-up lines or being anyone other than your true self. You're a man who women are attracted to. In fact, there were times during the last few days when we were talking to groups of them who were attracted to *you and only you*. You realize all that, right?"

"Yes."

I continued, "But if you don't have the discipline to go out every single day and do this, then you're just going to go back to the way you were before."

Another time, I was conducting a women's seminar and I broke down just how simple it is to meet men. I explained to the group that guys are really just giant Scooby-Doos on steroids. Picture the beloved animated dog when he's got a Scooby Snack in his sights—he's totally obsessed with that tasty treat until he gets it. That's exactly how all men are, because once they see a woman they're attracted to, they can't stop looking at her. I told the participants, "You're all giant Scooby Snacks, and all you need to do is be yourselves to attract your own Scooby-Doo!"

As the ladies in the audience were laughing and smiling, I went on: "That is the key to meeting men everywhere. If you can hold a smile and look at a man straight in the eyes, and if you can lose the rigid body language, be open and engaging, and not be a back-turner or a ground-looker, then you'll have him hooked."

■ ■ ■

Discipline is everything when it comes to meeting potential mates and having a great social life, because it shows that you're willing to go out there every day and leave your comfort zone. It means maintaining a confident and secure mind-set, and that whenever a negative thought comes into your mind, you'll squash it and not give power to it. So when somebody doesn't call you back, you need to have the discipline to introduce yourself to other people and not look back. And once you're able to display this quality consistently, you'll be able to love yourself every single day.

Discipline is the difference between someone who's successful and someone who's not. The most prosperous individuals have it, while those who struggle have minds that wander all over the place. They can't keep their focus on the task at hand because they get bored easily and, therefore, don't become great at anything. In order to find the most amazing relationship, you must be disciplined in every aspect of your search—from meeting someone to dating to your mind-set to simply having a conversation.

The one thing you need to remember is that without this vital attribute, none of what I'm teaching you will work in the long run. I can see you right now thinking, *No, David, I can do this. I really, truly want to go out there and meet an amazing man [or woman]. I can do this.*

The question is, how committed are you? Keep in mind that discipline and commitment are cousins. When you're committed it means you've got discipline, because you're devoted to the end result—which in this case is to go out there and find a loving relationship, or maybe even get married.

■ ■ ■

A woman came to one of my seminars with a friend. She didn't say a word the entire time, and I looked at her at the end and said, "You know, you've done nothing but nod your head, laugh, and agree with everything I said. You'd be the perfect client, and you're making me feel wonderful, but I know nothing about you. Are you just agreeing with me here today, and then you're going to go home and forget all about this?"

She replied, "No, David. I'm in love. I'm getting married. I just came here with my girlfriend. Everything you say makes sense, and it took me a lifetime to figure it all out."

My curiosity was piqued, and I asked her to tell me more.

"I am 47 years old and have never been married. Hell, most women my age would become cat collectors at this point. I've got a friend who's in her 50s, and she's on her fifth kitty. I didn't want to be called 'crazy cat lady' or come home to the sound of meows and the smell of a litter box. I wanted to meet a man. Yes, I know men might smell like litter boxes at times, but I'd much rather have a one of them than a creature that rubs against my leg one minute and then looks as if it wants to kill me the next. A lot of women would have given up by now, and I was one of them. Then I realized I lacked the commitment and discipline I needed to find the relationship I deserved."

I wasn't quite sure where she was going with her story, but at this point I was very interested. So she started to tell everybody about how in her 20s she was having fun and dating; in her 30s she got a new job, and her career took off; and in her early 40s she felt as if her time was up and the chance of finding a husband had passed her by. She wanted kids, but never had them. She wanted to get married, but couldn't find the right guy. All her friends called her picky. But what she finally realized—and admitted to herself—was that she lacked commitment to her relationships.

She looked back at her life and realized that she was dedicated to her career. She had the ability and determination to be successful, and she was one of the most outstanding people in her field because of her commitment, desire, and discipline, or CDD. (That's a lot better than ADD, isn't it?) So she decided to apply the same CDD to her relationships as she did to her professional life. She made a pact with herself to go out and meet men every single day. She made it her job to push herself, be aware of where men are, smile, say hello, and hand out her phone number if she was interested in a guy—even if he didn't ask her out.

She succeeded in meeting a lot of men. Some called and some didn't. She went out on a lot of first and second dates and suffered a lot of disappointment, but she was dedicated to stick with it the same way she did with her work. She had equal amounts of commitment, desire, and discipline.

Then one day, magic happened. She was at her dry cleaners. The man behind the counter greeted her and said, "Hey, there's a guy who comes in here all the time—he asked about you last week. He said he'd seen you here before but never had the opportunity to talk because you were always coming, he was always going, and he just didn't find the right moment. Can I hook you guys up?"

So this woman, being somebody who was committed and had desire and discipline, said, "Absolutely."

And how long did it take her to find the man of her dreams? It took her a couple years to build up the courage to really put herself out there, but then only ten months to meet the person she was going to spend the rest of her life with.

Take a minute to write down the level of commitment you have to finding a relationship. How much time per day can you give to this? What are you willing to do to step out of your comfort zone? Get it all down on a piece of paper. Are you prepared to hold yourself accountable? Start by taking 30 minutes out of each day to go out there and try to meet someone.

■ ■ ■

What do you think of when you hear the term *executioner?* Do you think of some scary guy in a hooded mask from the 1600s who's getting ready to take someone on a one-way trip to the gallows? Or do you imagine the film *The Green Mile,* in which an executioner is responsible for electrocuting a convicted murderer?

What if I told you that *you* need to become an executioner? Do you think you could play one of these roles? Lucky for you, that's not exactly what I'm saying. No, to me an executioner is someone who executes every single day. In other words, it's a person who makes engaging others a priority in his or her life.

To go out and force yourself to become a more social person—and meet that special someone—you've got to do several things. The first is that you've got to get your head out of your butt, your eyes off your iPhone, and become 100 percent aware of everything that's going on around you. I've always believed that meeting people naturally throughout an entire day is the key to success. Going out and doing so casually in supermarkets, coffee shops, elevators, and anywhere else just might find you someone to build a relationship with.

But you've got to become an executioner to be successful, because you need to understand the power of the Big Mo, otherwise known as momentum. When people don't have momentum in dating, it's like running a race but going nowhere fast. What happens is they take two steps forward—hopeful in making a connection with someone new—and then they immediately take two steps back, as their fears drag them right back to where they began, over and over again.

Here's an example of how this usually plays out: You go out on a date that you're all excited about, which is taking two steps forward. Everything goes well, but then you go home and talk to your third-base coach—that friend you always go to for relationship advice. You ask, "What did he mean when he said this to me?"

Your friend will reply, "I think *this* is what he meant." In reality, she has no idea what the guy's intentions were, because she's never met him! Asking her for advice has just taken you one step back. Then your date doesn't call, so you take another step back. You're back at the starting line, and you're asking yourself, *Should I even bother?*

Yes, you *should* bother. Take a step forward every single day, and you'll never see the starting line ever again. And, by the way, you won't see the finish line until the end of your life anyway. Just be content somewhere in the middle and be happy with the race that you're running.

■ ■ ■

I once had a client named Mark who booked me for what turned out to be a wonderful private weekend. He went out and met all different types of people during our time together and made a real effort to become a genuinely social person. We went through his list of what he wanted in life and the type of women he hoped to attract. We even changed his entire wardrobe, so he actually fit the part.

Mark's new style had him looking hip and trendy, instead of ultraconservative, because that's the kind of mate he wanted to attract. By the end of the weekend, my client had gotten two dates, and he was ecstatic about the outcome.

And then about a month later, Mark called me and said, "I've lost all my momentum."

"What happened?" I asked.

"I got lazy," he admitted. "I stopped doing it. I was on a roll for two weeks, and then I was really bad for a week and felt my old habits creeping back in. I had some unconfident days thrown in there, too."

"Do you remember the action plan we put together? Read it to me."

He dutifully recited it: "Go out every day and spend 15 minutes talking to people. When you're out and about and you see people you want to talk to, smile and say the first thing that comes to your mind. Speak with confidence and conviction. When you're interested in a woman you've actually enjoyed having a conversation with, ask her out. Don't get caught up on the outcome, because that's not what's important. It's all about going out there every single day and talking to people as you're running errands, sitting outside between meetings, or grabbing dinner. And as an added bonus for your action plan, you need to go out two nights a week by yourself, sit at a bar, and interact with the people around you."

There were a few more things in the plan, but I interrupted Mark right there. "This is your *action* plan. The first two weeks after we worked together, what did you do?"

"I followed it every day, and I felt great. I was striking up conversations all day long and building my social network; I even had a really friendly exchange with a married woman. A week later, I saw that same woman at the gym and got a date with her friend who was there with her. We both had a really good feeling talking to each other. Everything was great."

"So, what happened?"

"I don't know," he said. "I was doing fine, and then all of a sudden I wasn't. No one was really responding to me, and I began thinking, *What's wrong with me? Am I losing it?*"

I stopped Mark right there. "You weren't losing it. You were just having a bad day, which is perfectly okay. Everybody has them. We all have days when we're 'off,' when we're not in the mood to talk, and when we're not being very social or friendly. Remember, life is a stage, and sometimes the matinee needs to be canceled. Sometimes you need to hire a stand-in for a while. If you don't feel up to it one day, you never have a chance to make a first impression again. So just don't get onstage that day, and take a little time off."

That was also in his action plan, down by the bottom. But internally he had beat himself up, and that sent him into a bit of a downward spiral. So we talked a little more and I asked, "What do you think my answer is? Get back on the action plan!"

And that's what he did.

I called Mark a few months after to follow up, and his attitude had completely changed. "Dude, I've had the best three weeks of my entire life!" he told me. "It's been unbelievable—I'm introducing myself all day long, everywhere I go. I've got three more dates. One of the women I think I actually like a lot, and we've planned to go out on a second date."

When most people try to meet someone new, they use a particular approach, and if it doesn't happen to work they just stop, losing any momentum they might have had in the process. Here's the truth, folks: there's no magic pill. If you're a salesperson, you can call ten people and you might not get any sales. But you don't give up—you make ten more calls and keep working at it until you close some deals. You don't just shut down the shop.

When you talk to ten people in a social setting, three of them might be interested in talking with you, and seven may tell you to leave or go stick your head in the mud. (They're probably not going to be mean like that, but you get my drift.) The key is that you've got to form new habits, and the way to do so is to try something new.

I want you to come up with an action plan so you can become the most incredible, social person there is. You need to build momentum while you build your confidence one step at a time, because if you build momentum in life, you're bound to be successful.

In the NFL, how many times does the team with the momentum at the end of the season win the Super Bowl? A perfect example of this is the Green Bay Packers, who won in 2011. Going into the playoffs, they'd built enough momentum to win the rest of their games and become champions.

Life is all about momentum. Whatever you do, you need to build it by working on your dating career a little bit at a time. If you have a setback, look at it and say, "No big deal. These things happen." And make a pact with yourself to do something to meet people every day and *not* return to your old habits.

This is how you successfully gain momentum. And it has worked for every client I've ever coached, so you have no excuse. Remember: it takes commitment, desire, and discipline. When you've got that, a prosperous love life is sure to follow.

■ ■ ■

A key part of getting naked is understanding exactly what you want in life. In the next chapter, we'll determine exactly what that is.

■ ■ ■

CHAPTER 8

EMBRACE THE MAGIC OF WHO YOU ARE

Who do you desire?

I know there's probably a list of people you're thinking about right now. It could be the guy you've seen several times at your favorite breakfast place for the past six months, but you don't even know who he is.

Or maybe you've been noticing a woman at your gym who's on the treadmill a few evenings each week, and you wish you could just go over and talk to her. You're attracted to her because she looks like everything you've ever wanted—maybe more.

Considering who you desire right now can be a fun exercise, but let's take it a little further. What kind of person is right for you? Do you even know? Have you ever taken the time to really figure out who will make you happy? Have you ever created a list of everything you like, want, and desire in somebody?

Do you have any idea who you're searching for? A lot of people don't.

It's incredibly important for you to understand what you're looking for in a mate. Why? Because if you don't, 99 times out of 100 you're not going to have a great relationship.

Think about all of your past romances for a moment. Which ones worked on a long-term basis? Which ones didn't? What recurring patterns do you notice?

Next, take some time to consider your former partners. What type of individuals were you able to stay with for a long time? What did you have in common? Now, why did you two break up? What did he or she do that frustrated you? You need to consider whether or not someone ultimately made you happy, otherwise your dating situation isn't going to improve. Are there certain issues that seem to move your relationships from good to bad?

What exactly is it that you desire in a mate? Go deep into this—and write it all down.

Do you want someone to tell you that you're beautiful once a day? Do you need someone to profess his or her passion and desire for you? Do you require hugs and kisses—lots of them? Do you insist on receiving lots of affection? Do you like to have sex six days a week? Four days a week? Do you enjoy in-depth conversations? Do you want somebody to watch TV or movies with? I want you to record all your desires, but more important, I want you to prioritize them.

What are your four core desires? That is, what are the four things you can't live without in a mate? Recall your dating history. Now think about which relationships were able to hit two out of the four, three out of the four, or even all four out of four. I guarantee that if you look at your entire love life, these core desires are things that you learned through the school of hard knocks during the course of those past relationships.

And if you haven't had a boy- or girlfriend yet, read this chapter anyway, because it's going to teach you a lot that you'll need to know and be aware of once you do.

■ ■ ■

By understanding your desires, you have the opportunity to be more honest with your partner. I remember when I was in my 20s, and I was dating a woman who sexually frustrated me. We were great friends, but we just didn't connect at all in the romance department. I was bartending at that time, and there was another girl named Andrea who used to come into the bar all the time. The electricity between the two of us was incredible, but because I was having so much trouble being honest with myself, I wasn't able to end things with my girlfriend.

I was stuck.

Have you ever had so much trouble in a relationship that you wished the other person would just break up with you, because you don't have the guts to do it yourself? Well, that's exactly what was happening to me, and it was killing my ability to find and date the right woman.

It ended up taking me *months* to get that girl to break up with me. And in the meantime, Andrea, whom I desired and was excited by, lost interest and found someone else.

When you're dating, you've got to be honest and understand that if the person you're with isn't working out, it's best for the both of you to cut your losses and move on.

Personally, I'm very simple to be with. (Based on that last story, I know a lot of women are probably going to say, "No, that sounds complicated.") As people—card-carrying members of the human race—we can be very complex. However, we're also very basic in so many ways. We need to be loved. We need to be felt. We need to be able to go to our partners and say anything that's on our minds.

As you've probably figured out by now, I don't like to sweep things under the rug, even though that's the way I was raised. When I was a kid, I used to tell my friends to be careful as they walked into the Wygant house; otherwise, there was a good chance they'd trip on all of the things that had been swept under the doormat over the years. It was so bad that I swore I'd never let this kind of thing happen in my house when I grew up.

I can't stand that feeling when things are all bottled up—it makes me stressed. So when it comes to relationships, one of my greatest desires is to be heard by my partner. And I want to be able to go to her and talk about *anything.* If I feel like I can't do that—and *really* be heard—then I'm going to shut down. And when this happens, I get extremely frustrated.

But isn't frustration something I just have to accept in any relationship? you may be asking. No, and here's why that way of thinking is such a problem. When you get angry with your partner, the natural result is that you will eventually go into attack mode. These emotions will continue to build if the issues remain hidden and unaddressed. So by the time you finally do talk to your lover, the irritation you've been feeling overflows, and you end up lashing out. And if you do this on a regular basis, then you can be sure that the relationship is doomed.

I know that my partner and I will not always be in complete agreement—that's not the issue. What's important is that when there are things we disagree about, we've got to be able to talk about them openly and truthfully and work them out.

I want the person I'm with to know me, feel me, and be in tune with me; and I don't want to have to ask a thousand times for something. There are moments when I just want my head rubbed (doesn't everybody?). If our relationship is in sync, she's going to know that I love having this done to me every day and make an effort to please me without my asking. And, of course, I'll be aware of what she likes and do those things without her having to say anything.

It's important for me to be with that type of person, because I'll get very frustrated if I'm not. And a frustrated relationship eventually breaks down and falls apart.

I want to feel passion and desire for my partner—that's one of my needs. I also require a lot of intimacy, and I can't be with somebody who isn't like that as well. My lover should be my best friend as well—someone I can trust and honor, and who longs for the same thing in return. These things are very simple. I know what they are, and I know what I want.

■ ■ ■

A client of mine spent 17 years in a marriage, and he and his wife were *never* on the same page. They had two kids, but this guy felt as if he were the third child of the family based on the way his wife treated him—he was always letting her down for one reason or another. She would say over and over again how disappointed she was in him, and, as a result, he was never comfortable talking to her. He was always afraid that one of his comments would unleash another attack on his self-worth, but that didn't stop him from trying. He would make the effort to approach his wife in gentle ways: "I know I disappoint you, but I just wish we could have more sex and be able to discuss things more as adults."

Her response would invariably be along the lines of, "We'd have sex more often and talk more as adults if you didn't disappoint me as a person." For my client, this lack of communication was a lose-lose situation. It was as if he and his wife were speaking completely different languages.

So one day he got honest—with himself. He left his wife and began divorce proceedings.

A couple years later, my client met a woman and ended up in what turned out to be the *best* relationship he'd ever been in. And part of the reason why everything was so great was because he learned how to articulate his desires right from the get-go. He realized that the main reason both he and his ex-wife had been frustrated in their marriage was because neither one could express his or her own desires. There was never an open forum to talk, while each person simultaneously attempted to control the other.

As you can see, if you want to build a long-term, meaningful, committed relationship, you've got be willing to communicate your own desires while respecting and fulfilling your partner's.

Understand also that your needs don't have to be exactly the same as your lover's. As long as you're in the same ballpark, you can play. For example, I want someone who's very athletic—who likes to be active, stay in shape, and take care of her body. I love a woman who works out. Feeling her tight body and watching her work out is incredibly sexy to me. Those are my desires—that's how I'm wired. However, I don't expect her to necessarily be a gym rat like I am. She might like to spend a lot of time hiking, cycling, or roller-skating. That's fine. So long as she enjoys to exercise, I'm happy.

Honesty is a vital part of what I'm talking about—you must be completely transparent with everything there is to know about who you are and what you desire. This is the only way you'll ever truly know if you're with the right person or not, or if something is going to cause problems down the road. I understand that there are compromises in life. I may want Thai food when she wants Mexican, so we work it out. Or if she suggests we go on a beach vacation, and I prefer a big city, we can decide to go somewhere that offers a little of both.

We can and do readily compromise on our noncore likes and desires, but it's much more difficult to do so on core issues. If you find yourself in that situation, this is a red flag that you're not with the right person. It means that you didn't know, understand, or acknowledge your needs from the beginning. I know this because I've consistently made that mistake: I've been in relationships with people I knew wouldn't satisfy me from the very beginning. We simply weren't alike in those very essential ways.

If you are going to find someone with whom you're a great fit, you have to first match your desires. You can't hide your true self, as this will eventually reveal itself no matter how hard you try to keep it out of sight. Just be yourself. Understanding this idea is a very powerful lesson—and by putting it into practice, you won't clash with your lovers, and your relationships will be that much better. You'll inevitably find somebody who respects your desires, wants to make you happy, and really gets you.

■ ■ ■

One of my clients named Sophia was a fitness queen. She was always into working out and challenging herself to go farther, whether it was cross-country skiing, snowboarding, taking yoga classes, or whatever. Therefore, it was really important that she find a mate who enjoyed physical activity just as much as she did.

You can probably guess where this story goes next. She ended up with a great guy who *wasn't* into staying in shape. He was a weekend warrior, wasn't really into fitness, and worked out only when he felt he needed to. He was, however, *very* appreciative of the fact that Sophia was fit and trim and looked great. And while she loved his mind and who he was a person, physically she wasn't satisfied. Yet she kept the relationship going because she didn't want to seem shallow. In reality, her true desire was to be with someone who was both a workout partner and a lover.

Although Sophia wasn't happy, she stuck with this guy for years. Over time, he started gaining weight and getting lazier. She became increasingly frustrated and tried to do anything she could to get his butt to the gym. But he simply didn't want to go. While she realized that her boyfriend was wrong for her, she could hear her mother's voice saying, "You'll never find anyone who's perfect, so just be happy with who you're with."

But Sophia knew there had to be more. She so desperately wanted an athletic guy to do things with that she finally got the nerve to end the relationship. Her friends thought she was crazy—here she was at 40 years of age dumping a perfectly good man. They kept asking her where she thought she was going to find someone new. And, indeed, she did spend a couple of years alone. There were times that she worried, *Maybe they were right—what if I made a mistake.* She went out on dates and met guys who were athletic and fit but didn't have the substance that her ex did. She even began doubting herself, wondering if maybe there was no such thing as Mr. Right.

Then she met me. After working together for a few weeks, Sophia regained her confidence and a positive attitude. Six months after our initial session, she met the man she'd always been seeking, and today they're still together. They're out there skiing the world, running marathons together, and pushing one another to new heights—mentally and physically.

Desires are important in life, and if there's something that's vital in order for you to be happy, then don't give up on it.

Here's the deal about relationships: loving yourself is always the most important thing. To truly love someone else, you've got to first accept and embrace yourself. But this is the kicker: it will be imperative for you to listen to, learn, and want to understand your partner's desires. You've got to drop your ego so you can satisfy, and become more in tune with, his or her needs. Once you do, you'll see that this will create the most beautiful relationship in the world.

We all know how to love the way *we* want to be loved. But to truly do so and let go, to genuinely experience and embrace others, we've got to love our mates the way *they* need to be loved. We have to honor their desires. Doing so creates such a deep love, one where we can naturally go up to the person and understand exactly what he or she needs just from a facial expression.

The only way that's possible is if you understand your own desires. So embrace the magic of who you are, whatever that might be.

When you do this, you'll attract individuals whom you'll be able to communicate freely and openly with. You'll be able to listen carefully to what they need, and then satisfy them based on the goodness of your heart.

■ ■ ■

You've learned from "Chapter 2: The Law of Attraction in Dating" that life mirrors your words, thoughts, and attitudes. By speaking to people from your heart, you'll be rewarded tenfold. Expect that they already know what you love, want, and desire. This will lead you to a beautiful relationship, because two people who really want to experience this *will* find each other. And by understanding the depth of who you are as a person, you'll have the ability to clearly communicate your needs.

You know what you want. If you speak your mind with love and beauty, then your boy- or girlfriend will want nothing more than to make you happy. You are creating this amazing relationship because of what's required in order for it to succeed.

So, besides writing down all of your desires—which is so important to do—how else can you better understand if you and your potential mates are compatible or not? Well, I strongly suggest that after every date you take the time to assess how things went. As you replay the events and conversations in your mind, ask yourself these questions:

- Is this someone who can understand me?
- Is this someone who will respect my desires?
- Is this someone who seeks his or her own desires?
- Is this someone who speaks the truth, and from his or her heart?

Of course, it's nearly impossible for a potential lover to have every single thing that you're looking for. It doesn't work that way in the real world. Everyone is going to have issues, and you and your partners are going to have disagreements and even fights from time to time.

That's a normal part of being in a relationship. But after the battles are waged and you've gotten everything out into the open and dealt with it head-on, then the two of you must get back to fulfilling each other's desires.

The sooner you understand this, the sooner you'll stop repeating the negative themes that get in the way of long-term relationships. Believe me: you'll be more satisfied, and so will your mate.

If you take the time to identify and be clear about your needs, you'll be more sure about who you are, what you're about, and why you're entering into a particular relationship when it occurs; you'll start off knowing the important things that you require; and you'll be speaking from your heart, standing your ground, and practicing abundance. And if the person you're currently dating can't satisfy the core desires from the list you made at the beginning of this chapter and refuses to budge, you'll know with absolute certainty that you'll have to move on.

Being really satisfied with somebody is such an amazing and powerful experience. It's the safest feeling you're ever going to have. But for this to come true, you've got to get secure with yourself first. You have to make sure that you truly understand and embrace all that's important to you. I honestly believe you can find that really incredible someone who will fulfill your desires—and whose desires will be fulfilled by you. And you'll do so lovingly, without expecting anything in return. Be assured that once you reach this level, you'll actually get everything back and more, because you won't be keeping score.

Identify your list of four core desires, and then stand by them. Doing so requires learning how to speak honestly to yourself, and this is a topic we'll focus on in the next chapter.

■ ▇ ■

CHAPTER 9

COMMUNICATE WITH HONESTY TO YOURSELF

You can't fight your own truth.

Have you ever heard that before? To me, this means that every day when you wake up you need to be honest about how you feel, who you are, and what you want. It doesn't matter where you are in your life right now. You need to be 100 percent genuine with yourself in every aspect of your life—not just in dating, but also in relationships with friends, co-workers, and family members.

If being completely connected and honest with the way you feel about everything sounds stressful to you, then I'm sorry. Sweeping things under the rug is *not* allowed.

As I confessed to you earlier in this book, my family refused to deal with a lot of issues when I was growing up. I was always taught that if you aren't happy with something, you hide it. My go-to person was my mom, and my hide-everything-from person from was my dad. I was able to tell Mom the truth, but she of course didn't want to do that with Dad, so we always had these secrets.

Are you the kind of person who doesn't want to challenge others when you speak to them? Are you afraid that if you actually spoke your truth—that is, communicated honestly with yourself and your boy- or girlfriend—that your relationship would fall apart? And because of that fear, do you keep things repressed inside? By the time you go to talk to your partner, does so much anger come pouring out that he or she doesn't even want to be around you anymore? I've done that, and I'm definitely still guilty of it at times. I'll bottle up something inside, pull back, and take the love away from my mate.

After a couple of days of doing this, she'll get really frustrated, and I'll finally figure out that I've got to tell her what I'm feeling. I'm so happy that I'm finally speaking my truth that I blurt it all out—at this point, there's so much built up that it all just comes flooding out of me. But by then it's too late. If I had just been candid from the beginning and not concealed whatever was bugging me, I wouldn't have felt the need to dump everything on her all at once.

Successful dating requires learning how to speak honestly with yourself first, and then expressing that truth to others. I'm going to repeat something that I said at the beginning of the chapter: You can't fight your own truth.

■ ■ ■

I'd like to share another story with you about a wonderful woman I used to coach named Sasha. She did everything right in trying to get a particular man she was interested in to like her. She was being herself emotionally as well as sexually, and she was calling him at times—even though everybody says that the girl shouldn't being the one doing this—but the guy rejected her.

She e-mailed me afterward, asking, "What did I do wrong?"

I responded, "You did absolutely nothing wrong. You were honest, open, vulnerable, and real. He wasn't."

Sasha saw that I was right. "Oh my God, that makes so much sense. But what should I do next time?"

"Be open, honest, and real again. But remember that it might not work again the next time. And it may not work the next five, six, or seven times. But here's the reason why you've got to keep trying anyway: the only person you want it to work with is somebody who's like you—a guy who's in touch and honest with himself. You want a partner who can communicate truthfully with you; appreciate who you are; and speak openly about his needs, wants, and desires. This way you'll feel safe with him. After all, who wants to be in a relationship where you're walking on eggshells? That only adds stress to your life, and it's not healthy."

Sasha immediately got what I was saying: "If I do this over and over again until I meet the right person, then what you're telling me is that when I find the right person, I'm going to forget about all the others?"

"Exactly!" I affirmed. "Because all those other experiences were just to teach you how to be open and honest and help you find the right man."

It's such a powerful thing to be 100 percent honest with yourself and your prospective partner—when you decide *not to* play the role of Mr. or Ms. Agreeable on a date. If the person sitting across from you says he loves water-skiing but you don't, you're not going to say "I love it, too!" and be miserable while you're spending your weekends being pulled behind a boat.

Or if that cute girl you're out to dinner with tells you that her dream is to have three children—and you don't want any—you're not going to pretend to agree, thus getting into a relationship based on a lie. If this is how things start off, it's pretty much guaranteed that they'll eventually go bad because you won't have the life that *you* want. Instead, you're fulfilling *someone else's* dream, *someone else's* desires. *Wow* . . . think about being a passenger in someone else's life. Isn't it more fun taking turns behind the wheel?

And what's worse is that when you get into a situation that was built on a lie, there's no way your mate is going to be able to live his or her truth freely. Why not? Because the two of you will be arguing and fighting every step of the way as a result of your conflicting interests or goals. To use the two previous examples, you'll be depriving your partner of participating in an activity he loves (water-skiing), and he'll be keeping you from starting the family you always wanted.

Those are just a couple of examples.

It could also be about where you want to live. If you'd really like to live in the city, but your boy- or girl-friend prefers the suburbs, then you've got a fundamental disconnect. If you decide to give in and move to the suburbs to make your partner happy, you're not even compromising. You're living his or her life, and this is the type of sacrifice that you just can't make.

No matter how hard we try, it's impossible to force a square peg into a round hole, right? We learned that simple lesson in kindergarten. So now as adults, we must stop attempting to be someone we're not.

■ ■ ■

I'm a big believer in using a personal journal to help you keep track of your emotions and learn to communicate honestly. Here's a good way to put your journal to work for you. Every day, take some time to write down how you feel about yourself. Make a note of how well you connected with others, how you felt when your boss yelled at you, and what went through your mind when a potential partner turned you down. Habitually write everything down as you learn to express yourself sincerely.

And when you return home after a date, use your journal to recount the experience. Are there conflicts in your respective wants and needs that might cause long-term problems in a relationship? Put down the things that could potentially create issues, such as kids, hobbies, and lifestyle choices. The sooner you do this, the sooner you'll touch base with these feelings, and the sooner you'll be able to leave behind the negatives and move forward with the positives.

Everyone seems to think that if they just get a little more, their lives are going to be great. How many people do you know who aren't content with where they are, convinced that if they got more of something—more money, more toys, more sex—they would finally be satisfied? I'll bet you know plenty, maybe including yourself.

Look, where you are in your life right now is exactly where you need to be. This means that whatever your current dating situation is in this moment is precisely as it's supposed to be. So embrace it.

If you're alone, single, and not great at meeting the opposite sex, then maybe your truth is that you need to get better at finding a potential mate. Doing so, however, may require that you first improve your understanding of who you are. You must work on becoming comfortable with yourself, so you're able to converse openly and not feel like you have to be Mr. or Ms. Agreeable. When you communicate honestly with yourself, you'll begin to see who you really are. Then, when you go out and meet prospective partners, you'll be less needy and more resistant to giving your power away.

You want to pick the next person instead of being picked. You don't want to date somebody just because you're afraid to be alone and agree to be with whoever chooses you. That relationship isn't going to work.

As I mentioned, I wandered down that road when I was in my 20s. I went out with someone who wanted to be with me, and things weren't right from the get-go. But I was sick and tired of being single, so I decided to go out with the woman who showed an interest in me. It was a huge mistake at the time, but I learned from it and moved on.

And you can, too.

It's time you communicated honestly with yourself in every way. So start using your journal to express your truths. Write down how you feel. After you touch base with your emotions, that's when you're going to be able to leave behind the negatives in your life and carry on with the positives. And don't forget to go as deep as you can—into those intimate places and emotions within you.

■ ■ ■

In the next chapter, we'll discuss how to get to the truth of your intimacy.

■ ■ ■

CHAPTER 10

GET TO THE TRUTH OF YOUR INTIMACY

How intimate are you? How sexual of a person are you? How passionate are you? Are you somebody who loves to light candles, turn on some music, cook your favorite recipe, and open a bottle of wine to get your lover in the mood? Do you like to set an incredibly romantic and sensuous ambience for your partner, and require that he or she do that for you, too?

It's important to understand your desires. And I'm not just talking about making love—this goes much deeper than that. It gets at the heart of what you like and what you're willing to do.

Do you enjoy discussing sex? Are you into talking dirty? Do you prefer to be on top or bottom? Are you into oral sex—giving and receiving? Are you kinky? Do you like to dress up for your mate? Do you like to masturbate in front of him or her? How do you feel about phone sex? Do you like to make love three times a week, four times a week?

These are all questions that you need to consider, and it's what we're going to dig into right now. Intimacy is a very powerful thing, and all people have a distinct point of view about what that is. As you discover the truth about your own desires, you're going to be able to go out and meet someone who fulfills them and makes you happy.

Have you ever been in a relationship where the person you're with just doesn't seem to want to have sex as much as you? Does he or she never want to light candles or take bubble baths? Does your partner not want to kiss very much, lavish you with affection, or make you feel special? Remember: a relationship is a two-way street, and it's not just women complaining about men who don't make romance a priority. A lot of men are deprived as well.

Intimacy is something that's different for each one of us—there's no right or wrong way to show it. The problems begin when partners' ideas of it are totally at odds. For some people it's having really rough sex once a week—that's who they are. Others think quickies are fun, while some couples enjoy and prefer to have long, erotic lovemaking sessions. In my mind, there's nothing better than being able to crawl into bed with somebody who I'm absolutely head-over-heels in love with, and have fun all night long. It's exciting to be able to bring pleasure to someone; and to be able to see, feel, taste, and touch them. I love being able to look into someone's eyes as we make love and really connect deeply on all levels.

What I just described for you is the way *I* like to be intimate. I love romance; rubs; lighting candles at night; taking bubble baths with my partner; having long, passionate talks where I can look into her eyes; nice music; and having a long, incredible, hot session of passionate sex. That's who I am, and that's what I enjoy. But you certainly have your own idea of what's romantic for you. In order to make your relationships work, you have to be 100 percent confident about your intimacy—your wants and desires.

■ ■ ■

A woman named Madison attended one of my seminars a few years ago. She's what I call a "romance-novel queen." She truly believed in real-life romances, and she wanted to experience the grandest one of all. Madison loved being surprised with a gift, having bubble baths drawn for her, getting her toenails painted by her lover, letting a man light candles and set up a romantic evening, and looking and feeling really pretty for her special someone when they went out for a nice evening together.

By day, this woman had a very successful career, but she wanted to feel like a princess and make her man feel like a king. Unfortunately, Madison could never find a guy who felt the same way she did. After being frustrated countless times, she decided that guys were just insensitive to her needs. Her experience was that during the wining and dining stage they would do those things to make her happy, but then all of a sudden—after the honeymoon period was over, usually about six months into it—the romance would fade. This would inevitably leave her feeling empty, lonely, and unsatisfied inside.

Her friends tried to explain that this was just how things work—people become lazy and get used to one another. Eventually, the thrill goes out of any relationship. But she'd argue, "I want romance, and I don't believe I should have to compromise and let this desire die, because my soul needs to be fed."

So Madison kept breaking up with her boyfriends. Everyone thought she was crazy, because many of these men seemed like really good catches. She'd always say: "He may be a great guy, but he's not *my* great guy. My man will understand my needs, my desires, and my intimacy; and we'll be able to satisfy each other. We'll be able to romance each other. My parents have it—I see it in the way they hold hands—and I want it, too."

So she held out . . . and then held out a little longer. Finally, she came to one of my seminars about better understanding men, and did she learn *a lot!* At the end she asked me, "David, do you think I'm crazy?"

I replied, "No, I think you're an absolutely beautiful woman who believes in the power of romance, and that is a wonderful thing. You're not demanding diamonds, and you're not angling for him to buy you expensive gifts. You're asking to be loved in the way that you really want to be loved. You're asking for intimacy and sex the way you like it. And you're willing to give all these things in return. There are guys out there who appreciate that. But you need to be really clear in what you want and make sure you hold that thought and energy in order to be able to eliminate potential mates a little quicker so you don't get disappointed after six months."

Madison took my advice, and I told her to keep in touch. Two years later I got an e-mail from her, reporting that she was getting married to a great man who was one of the most romantic people she'd ever met. I congratulated her and asked how she persevered through all the breakups and failed relationships. She said, "Because you told me to believe. You made me realize that my desires, wishes, and needs shouldn't be sacrificed when it came down to it, that they were worth holding out for. Your advice really resonated with me and showed me that these are things I deserve. So I eliminated guys a lot faster. I went through them so quickly that sometimes my head would spin. And then I knew when Mr. Right came along, because we kept doing things for each other unconditionally. I'd light candles one night, and he'd light them the next. I drew a bubble bath for him, and he'd give me a massage. Not every night was perfect, but we did enough to make each other feel special and amazing."

Madison held out for the level of desire and passion she longed for. And you can hold out for exactly what you want, too. You might read this story and think, *Oh God, I don't want that. What a pain! It's too much work.* Or you might sigh and realize, *That's exactly what I want.* Either way, intimacy is different for everyone, and it's up to you to figure out what will make you happy.

■ ■ ■

In the pages that preceded this one, I've asked you to get naked, raw, open, and vulnerable. I did this because I know that those individuals who have done so are truly in love with themselves and will not care what other people think or say. They won't worry because they're completely satisfied with who they are.

When I first sat down to write this book, I knew I'd share my deepest thoughts with you. I'd tell you the way I like to do things and give you some of my most effective weapons. By putting a book out there that I hope a million or more people will read, I know that the world is going to learn some things about me that are very private. That being said, you're welcome to make judgments about me, but I want you to relate what you read back to your own life. Nobody's making judgments about you except *you.* Because I'm completely secure and in love with who I am, I'm able to share anything about my life and allow you to form whatever opinions you'd like. You even know what I'm like sexually and what I desire. That, to me, is the ultimate in openness, as I really am naked to the world. My most honest thoughts are open for anyone—and everyone—to see.

When you really make love to someone, you're 100 percent emotionally and physically naked. You don't think about anything except what you're experiencing with him or her in that moment. It's beautiful to be able to feel that with your partner. And by me sharing this with you, I'm naked . . . and you can be as well.

When it comes down to understanding your own intimacy, it's really important to know what you need so you won't become frustrated. As you know, some of the things couples tend to fight about are kids, money, and sex—or lack of these things—and a lot of relationships end due to intimacy issues. The reason why is because each person didn't really know—and was without love and respect for—him- or herself.

Some partners stay together way too long, because they're afraid to leave even after they realize that they're not meant to be. And that's exactly the reason why this work is so important right now. If you can stay naked, are clear about your intimacy, and know what satisfies you sexually, then the next time you meet somebody and he or she doesn't respond positively to your needs, you're not going to stay and waste your time.

Here's an exercise you can do right now to get a handle on your intimacy. Make a list of all your past relationships and note if there were lovemaking issues with any of them. Were your previous lovers aligned with and willing to fulfill your romantic desires the way you wanted? Was the sex what you wanted? Or was it a problem in your relationship? Were the warning signs written on the wall and you were just wishing that these individuals would become what you wanted them to be, instead of accepting who they really are?

■ ■ ■

A few years ago I was coaching Mike, a guy who happened to be in a serious relationship. The woman he was with was caring, sweet, and nice, but my client was physically frustrated in so many different ways. Sex with her, he told me, was a planned event. It was always on Saturday night at 10:00, for 15 minutes, and that was it. She'd come over during the week, and depending on how tired she was, they would make love—so long as it didn't infringe upon her rigid bedtime of 10:00 P.M. Romance was never a passionate and drawn-out event, and it was never spontaneous. It was just sex.

But Mike continued to stay with this woman even though he was unsatisfied. Why? Because he didn't think he would meet anybody else—he lacked an abundance mind-set. So he accepted the fact that he would never have the intimate relationship he desired.

During one of our sessions, I looked at him and asked, "Why do you live your life like that? Do you really want to continue on the path of being sexually unfulfilled, without the passion and desire that you crave?"

Mike replied, "I just feel that if we break up, there may not be anybody else after her."

So he and I worked together on his sense of lack and exactly what it was that he wanted. But most important, we attempted to enable him to let go of whatever was frustrating him and move on.

Soon after our session, Mike ended things with his girlfriend and started going out and meeting new people. In fact, he ended up finding *a lot* of potential mates. And it's funny—he told me he had amazing connections and off-the-charts intimacy with every woman he was with. He was able to have the type of sex he was missing in his last relationship. Things started to happen as if by magic—like a switch got turned on—all because he was clear about what he wanted.

■ ■ ■

What exactly do *you* want?

Write down who you are and what you like regarding intimacy. How do you like to have sex? What are your fantasies? What are your fetishes? What are your needs and desires? Describe the type of sex that you like to have in the kind of detail that gets you turned on while thinking about it.

The point of doing this activity is for you to meet somebody who will satisfy you in exactly that way.

I want you to become *the* most powerful romance writer in the entire world. The more detailed you are, the more you get to know yourself on this level, and the more you fall in love with yourself. In this way, you'll start attracting the kinds of people who are also turned on by what you've written.

You're not going to get involved with lovers who frustrate you anymore, and you're not going to meet the people who don't want to engage you in the kind of conversations you enjoy.

I invite you to share with me any of the exercises from this chapter. I will actually read each and every one of them—it's how I become a better coach. You can even send me something anonymously if you like. But whatever approach you decide to take, I would love to be able to understand the way you feel and how you want others to make you feel.

Ultimately, you need to ask yourself this question, which is part of the first exercise: Have your intimacy and sexual needs ever been totally satisfied? If so, how long has this lasted?

This chapter is really important because it's the one that's going to help you define who you are and what you need in a relationship.

To that end, I'd like you to do one final exercise before we go on to the next chapter. Write down what your most romantic night would be. Don't hesitate at all here. Be so open and so honest that this will really get to the core of your very being. Do this because you don't want to feel frustration any longer. You want to look at your next partner and think, *This is the best lover I've ever had in my life.*

Remember, you're entitled to all of this. You deserve to have the most incredible, fantastic love life that you could possibly imagine. You're worthy of being with somebody who wants to be with you just as bad. If you have an insatiable sex drive, then you need to be with someone who's wired the same way—where your craving and hunger for each other is so unbelievable that you can't wait to look in each other's eyes, feel one another, and rip each other's clothes off.

If that's who you are, then that's what you deserve. So if you're the kind of person who just likes to go home and have quickies at the end of the day, then find somebody who does, too. But get to know what you want on this level. It will be the most satisfying and amazing feeling in the world because you won't ever lack again in this area of your life. After all, if you have a great sex life, your relationship is going to be far more relaxing and complete than you ever imagined.

■ ■ ■

Of course, once you're in command of what it is that you want—and have gone as deeply and intimately as you can go—you've got to be able to communicate this to your partner. That's the topic that we'll explore in detail in the next chapter.

■ ■ ■

CHAPTER 11

LEARN TO SPEAK FROM YOUR HEART

Imagine for a moment that there's a national holiday called Speak From Your Heart Day.

On this very special day, from the minute you wake up in the morning a magic spell is cast over you. Now, this isn't just any old magic spell—it's similar to the one that Jim Carrey experienced in the film *Liar Liar*. From the moment you get out of bed until the time you fall asleep at night, you're only able to speak honestly and from your heart, truthfully saying what you feel in every situation.

We all know the games we play inside our heads: twisting someone's words around; stopping ourselves in midsentence; not expressing what we want and then leaving a room frustrated, annoyed, and angry because we didn't get what we wanted or are afraid of what others think. Allowing ourselves to behave in this way is a real problem, and it can do a lot of harm to our relationships.

So just suppose that there is one day each year when fairies sprinkle pixie dust on the world and only the truth comes out of everyone's mouths. And no one would be able to say anything hurtful, because I truly believe most people have really good hearts and don't want to intentionally hurt others. We have no choice but to be straightforward and honest and cut through the smoke-screens that we use in many of our typical conversations.

Can you imagine if you walked into a coffee shop on that magical morning, and sitting there was a woman you were instantly attracted to? And the minute you laid eyes on her you noticed that she was striking, was sexy, and had such an incredible energy about herself—and you just had a feeling that there was something very different and interesting about her.

Now envision yourself approaching this beautiful woman—because, don't forget, she's very receptive due to having had the same pixie dust sprinkled all over her that morning—and saying, "Look, I've got to tell you something. I walked in here, and your energy was unreal. Your smile lit up the room, and I just needed to come over here and figure out who you are. I'm curious about you."

She listens really carefully to your words, studies your face, and can see that you're speaking from the heart. So what is she going to do in that situation? She's going to look at you and reply, "Wow, I'm blown away by that! You just made me feel really good. You noticed my energy—I thought that was really cool." And the conversation would go on from there.

Imagine that your entire day was like that from beginning to end—all about experiencing people, being honest and up-front, and appreciating others for who they are deep inside. My God, it would probably be the best day of your life. Work would be unbelievable. Deals that you'd been working hard on would suddenly be agreed upon simply by calling your contact at the other company and saying, "All right, what are we doing? Let's come to a solution we're both happy about instead of continuing with this song and dance."

You go home that evening and get ready for the evening, because you've decided you're going out with someone you met earlier in the day. You don't wait a couple days to call, and then a few more days to see her. You're so excited to see this person, and simply can't deny what you're feeling. And when you meet, you two will have an open, honest, heartfelt conversation—after all, today there's no other choice.

What you're *not* going to do is call your friends and ask them what you should or shouldn't say or do on the date. All of those typical questions you've always asked when you're nervous—"When should I kiss her?" "What if I want to invite her up at the end of the night?" "Will I look anxious?" "Will I look desperate?" "Will I look like I only want sex?"—won't interest you in the least. You're simply going to go out, have an amazing time, and have a first kiss that happens at the perfect moment and comes from the heart.

It's just amazing. You're touching each other's hands, you're smiling, you're laughing. You're not agreeing with each other at every little turn because you're desperate or needy. You're challenging one another, having real conversations, and talking without fear, as if you were catching up with an old friend.

And then all of a sudden—while everything is going great—the clock strikes 12, and the pixie dust blows away and disappears. So now what happens?

Well, as you're sitting there, your mind allows thoughts of insecurity to seep back in: *Oh, my God. I'm starting to feel anxiety again. I wonder if she is really having a good time like me. What is she thinking? Should I really have told her about my uncle being in prison? Maybe she'll [he'll] think I'm an ex-con, or worse. I've got to excuse myself and go to the bathroom.*

And all that self-doubt begins to flood back in and penetrate your thoughts. You instantly get really worried: *While I'm in the bathroom, I should just call my best friend, go through the date with him, and see if he thinks that I've said anything wrong or misinterpreted my date's reaction.*

As a result, you've stopped speaking from your heart. And remember, whenever you come from a place of fear, things quit working, and you won't be able to have any type of a successful long-term relationship. But when you learn to express your feelings, you begin to embrace who you truly are and realize that there's never a need to give away your power.

So once you're able to naturally return to the state of mind that this magic holiday put you in, you won't go seeking acceptance. You won't have to think about what you're going to say before you approach somebody, and you'll go on dates simply being yourself. You can be comfortable just reacting to the world around you, making comments in inquisitive, innocent ways, based on observations. You then listen and react without fear or pretense. You do this because you are genuinely interested in someone and want to get to know that person better.

That's what life and speaking from your heart is all about. Because then you'll form real connections—where you and your date can't wait to see each other again. What I'm going to tell you right now is not going to shock you or blow you away. In fact, it's something you've experienced over and over again: even if you've convinced a potential mate that you're someone you're not, eventually the *real* you is going to show up.

■ ■ ■

I want to share with you a story that really means a lot to me. Years ago, I kept hoping that I would have my pixie-dust moment—one where I could naturally speak from my heart. And this is one of the greatest lessons when it came to meeting people and being honest. It happened on a really cold day in Boulder, Colorado. It was springtime, but in this part of the U.S. the weather tends to get a little iffy at times, even when it's not supposed to.

Anyway, I was on my way home from a two-hour massage and decided to stop at the market to pick up dinner. As I was paying, a beautiful woman walked into the store. She gave me a really big smile, and I immediately wondered if it had been directed at me. I quickly looked behind me and didn't see anyone, so I turned to face her and returned the gesture, only to have her smile at me again! At that moment, I did what everybody does—I left the store. I got in the car, put the keys in the ignition, backed up, and then stopped. I asked myself, *What are you doing? This is ridiculous. There's a woman who walked in there, smiled warmly at you twice, and now you're driving home! So now what? You're just going to go home and think about her and what you could have said or done?*

So I reparked the car and walked back inside.

I headed in the direction the woman had gone, and soon found her in the produce section putting some lettuce into her cart. I walked right up to her, she smiled, I smiled, and then I asked, "Have you got a minute?"

She replied, "Absolutely."

"I have to tell you something. When I first saw you a few minutes ago, you smiled at me. I thought maybe you were looking at somebody else, but now I'm pretty sure it was for me. I knew that if I didn't come talk with you right now, I'd be thinking about you later and wondering what I could have said or why I didn't approach you. Basically, I would have beaten myself up for months about the missed opportunity. So here I am."

She held out her hand and introduced herself . . . and we ended up spending four of the next five days together, since she happened to be on vacation. We had a great time together, and it really taught me something about the power of speaking from my heart. I learned that revealing my true feelings could open doors I never imagined.

No matter what act you try to put on, or what masks you wear to try to hide the real you, eventually you're going to get tired of being someone you're not. And your true self *will* show up and be on full display. So if you aren't transparent from the beginning and don't believe in who you are, then your date is going to see right through your facade. If you play it safe, and don't challenge each other or clarify things from the beginning, you're both going to be in for a big surprise.

Now your mate is suddenly wondering who this new you is, you're becoming frustrated, and neither of you are happy or satisfied. And you can probably guess what happens next: you're dealing with the heartbreak of one more relationship that didn't work out.

Speak from your heart. You don't need magic or pixie dust to do this. I hate to use this cliché, but you only live once, and none of us has any idea how long we'll be on this planet. So stop hiding behind a personality of acceptance and instead accept yourself for who you are.

Think about it.

■ ■ ■

When you go out and casually meet a bunch of cool people, do you stop being you? Do you try to sell yourself, giving them a watered-down version? Of course you don't! I can pretty much guarantee that you speak from your heart and get to know them in a very real way. When you meet somebody you want to be friends with, you don't call your closest friend and say, "Listen to this. I think I just found a new best friend today, so your time with me will be limited right now. Actually, there's a really good chance that you and I won't be best friends anymore, because I met this other person. You better go out there and find a new one."

No!

You don't act differently when you meet someone new whom there's no chance of having a romantic relationship with—whether they're the same sex as you or not—and start watering down your personality. Even if you've just found your new best friend, there's never a reason for you to be someone other than who you really are.

And that's how it should be when you meet your next girl- or boyfriend. You need to be yourself and speak from your heart. It's the only way to attain true self-acceptance, and it's what you must do to attract the right people into your life and develop healthy long-term relationships.

Here's an exercise I'd like you to do. Get out your journal and write down *everything* you want to say to all of the important people in your life. If you've always wanted to have that honest conversation with your parents, put down what you want to say to them. Think about the key points that you want to get across. Don't draft a detailed script, since life doesn't work that way. After all, the second you start talking, the other person is going to react, and the conversation will naturally flow as it's supposed to.

I once had a client named Reuben who was really nervous about an upcoming date. So he came to me beforehand and said, "Listen, David. I'm going to go out with this amazing woman. She's the girl of my dreams."

I asked, "How do you know that? Physically she might be right for you, but that's really just your penis and your eyes talking. Your brain can't possibly know if she's the perfect person because you don't really know her yet, and your heart can't be sure either. So your brain and your heart have to get together and ignore what your penis and your eyes are telling you."

Reuben looked at me and replied, "Can you help me think of some things to talk about?"

"No, I don't want to go through a mock conversation. I want you to simply get to know her. Notice how she reacts to the waiter. Pay attention to the way she smiles when she tells stories. Is work a positive or negative thing for her? Does she describe her exes in a friendly way, or does she bash them? Really listen to and learn about her, and share everything with her just as you would with one of your friends."

At that point, Reuben got very belligerent. He desperately wanted me to go through the date with him. He was angry, and he kept trying to re-engage me, desperately wanting me to help him create a script, but I sent him on his way.

But before I did, I gave him some final advice: "Speak from your heart tonight. Pretend you're talking to an old friend—somebody you've known forever and couldn't wait to see again and catch up with. Just have that mind-set."

I made him type that into his BlackBerry, so he could look at it again before his date. And if he had to excuse himself five times to go to the bathroom for a reminder, fine. I just wanted him to stay 100 percent present during the entire date.

Reuben called the very next day, and initially I wasn't sure if he'd be in a good mood or upset, or if he was able to get past all his insecurities and self-doubt.

"I had the best date I've ever had in my entire life!" he revealed. "It was unreal. I was so relaxed because I read what you told me—not once, not twice, but about 100 times. I was totally calm, and I didn't care what my date thought about me. I decided I was going to stop giving my power away and start speaking what I felt. So I did things completely differently than I ever have before, because I realized that what I've been doing has never worked out well. I'm actually seeing her again today, since I decided just to blurt out what I was feeling and ask her out again!"

Reuben has been with this same girl ever since. And if that's not a great "happily ever after" story, then I don't know what is.

■ ■ ■

Did you make that list of conversations you want to have with the important people in your life? If not, then do it now. Write down all the things you want to say to them—the important issues and the not-so-important issues. You know what they are. Maybe you and your brother aren't getting along right now and you miss him. Maybe there are some things that are really bothering you, like the way that he and his wife treated your mother during the holidays last year. Whatever it might be, add it to your list.

Of course, once you're done, you need to do something about all these people and items. Start by talking with the name at the top, and do so from your heart about whatever issues have been on your mind. Use your journal to guide the discussion, but be flexible enough to allow the individual to respond and bring up his or her own points. Make sure that, even if you get interrupted, you maintain sincerity and calmly get your point across, saying that you want to get everything out into the open so you clear your energy.

By creating this space and addressing your friends or family members, you can begin to move forward with your life, instead of constantly looking in the rearview mirror. All this garbage from your past does nothing but keep you stagnant in the present anyway. You can't have a successful dating life now while you're fretting over your past relationships, old bosses, or anyone else who continues to deplete your energy. And many times when you bring frustration and existing issues into new relationships, your partners become your therapists as they try helping you through your problems.

■ ■ ■

Isn't it funny how when we're not getting along with our partner, we'll talk honestly and frankly to our friends about what's irritating us? But then, when we sit down face-to-face with the person we love and lay out everything that's on our minds, we usually get cut off because we're not communicating authentically, and then the issues get left unresolved.

The net result is that we get more and more frustrated as the relationship remains stuck, all because we're so afraid to speak from our heart and nervous about what our mate is thinking and feeling. We simply don't want to get hurt, cause pain to another, or be misinterpreted.

Here is the sad and somewhat ironic thing about not being able to speak from your heart: First, you're actually hurting your loved one because you're not revealing your true self—you're hiding things that will one day come back to bite you. Second, it's guaranteed that your true intentions will then be confused as less than honorable.

When you're being totally honest, you'll be interpreted 100 percent correctly, because the other person will notice your sincerity and believe you. He or she may even see how much effort you're putting into the conversation, thus feeling empathy and listening even more intently.

This is something you can and should practice before you find your next girl- or boyfriend. Practice speaking from your heart with everyone you meet, all the time. When you run into a friend on the street, speak from your heart. When you talk to your boss, brother, or sister, speak from your heart. When you're at a store talking to a salesclerk or cashier, speak from your heart. When you are at a bar after work and meet someone new, speak from your heart.

When you do so, people feel you. And the result is a deeper connection with anyone from the get-go— whether it's someone you'll interact with for only a few minutes or someone you'll live with for the rest of your life.

Keep in mind that certain relationships aren't meant to last forever. Some end weeks, months, or even years before you think they're supposed to. In reality, many of them will end before they really get off the ground, and we must realize that this is the way things are supposed to be.

Speaking from the heart is the only way you're going to be successful in every aspect of your life. Starting today, make the commitment that whenever you're searching for a new relationship or are on a date with someone you're interested in, you'll fully embrace who you are. That way there will be no misconceptions or frustrations. And then you'll find the partner of your dreams and live the life you deserve.

As I wrote this book, everything transferred to these pages directly from my heart. I have exposed myself to you in so many ways, and there are still plenty of chapters left for me to show you so much more. As each one unfolds, I'll be coming more and more from my authentic self, because I absolutely believe everything I've written here. I've done all the exercises and suggestions, and I've had to figure things out the hard way on many occasions. I'm still discovering new techniques every day, but the most important one I've learned is to speak from my heart with everyone I meet, and it's an amazing and never-ending learning process to really embrace this.

■ ■ ■

In the next chapter, we'll explore how to create a very powerful dating tool: the video journal.

■ ■ ■

CHAPTER 12

CREATE A POWERFUL VIDEO JOURNAL

Think about this for a minute: life is a giant stage, and *you* are the master of your own performance.

Let me put this idea into more practical terms. You are living a full-length feature film each and every day. You are (of course) the star of this movie, and all the other people you interact with play different roles. Some have leading parts, some supporting, and many more are just extras—populating the background of the scenes from your life.

Now think about a recent Hollywood blockbuster that you either took the time to see in a theater or watched at home. The actors in that film are well-paid experts of their craft. They are extremely self-aware of their presence in each and every scene they're in. They know they have just a few minutes, or even seconds, to make an impression on the public, and you can bet they're doing everything they can to capture your attention and interest. That's why the casting director picked them for the job—to draw you into their performance so you'll hopefully tell your friends to go see the movie, too.

As the star of your own film, you can—and should—be just as self-aware of the impression you're making on those you're interacting with. Are you performing like the star you are—demanding the attention of those around you—or are you simply behaving like an extra, hiding in the background and hoping no one will notice you?

Truth be told, many of us don't actually know the answer to that simple but telling question. Why? Because we aren't self-aware.

Self-awareness is one of the keys to finding the rewarding, long-term relationship that you want and deserve. The individuals who are in tune with how they come across are the ones who are out there making new acquaintances and creating deeper, more meaningful bonds with the people they already know. Those who are less sensitive to their influence are the ones sitting home at night, cruising the Internet and hoping to find somebody . . . anybody.

The good news is that you can learn the chops that will turn you into an A-list star in the film that is your life. You'll be the kind of person others want to meet and get to know better, and you'll attract more of the potential mates you're interested in. I don't care if you're shy, nervous, anxious, or lack self-assurance and confidence. We're going to get rid of all that baggage and send it on a one-way flight to Tierra del Fuego, where you'll never see it again.

It's time to kiss it good-bye.

■ ■ ■

I've long known that video is an especially powerful medium. As the old saying goes, a picture is worth a thousand words. It may be old and cliché, but it's true. Who hasn't been affected by a story he or she has seen on the network evening news? Video has the power to move people. It records them at their best and worst, and now it can be broadcast around the world in just minutes.

But I didn't appreciate its true power until I started putting my dating movies on YouTube three years ago (check out my channel, called "The Naked Truth About Dating, Sex, and Relationships" at: **www.youtube.com/ user/davidwygant**). Back then, uploading content on YouTube involved taking a huge leap of faith. You'd post your video and not know if anyone would ever see it; or, if someone did, whether or not he or she would even care.

That was then, and this is now. After putting my first video on the site, I've attracted more than eight million views. Yes, you read that right: eight *million* freaking views. A lot of people's lives are being changed by those videos. But what is it exactly that compels them to take the time to actually watch? Sure, they're seeking answers to the long-standing question of how to find, meet, and date the perfect partner. But beyond that, they're enjoying my performance—the way that I inhabit that little player on their computer screen.

And that's the real beauty of video. If you let it, a movie can provide you with a unique opportunity to see yourself as others do—physical warts, behavioral tics, confidence gaps, and all. You probably have countless photos of yourself, but those alone won't take you to the place you need to go. They're just two-dimensional snapshots of a particular place and time, lacking any context or action. Videos, on the other hand, give you a whole different dimension—they provide who you are and how others see you, and they do it in real time. This information is remarkably helpful when it comes to figuring out how to become a better actor in the film of your life.

The heart of the problem is this: our brains are naturally wired to filter out the barrage of information we're bombarded by each and every day—with only a small percentage entering our conscious thought. We hear, see, and feel the things that are familiar to us and that match up with our concept of the world, and we simply don't recognize the rest. People naturally read, watch, and experience things in a way that reinforces their self-concept. In reality, the way we see ourselves is rarely the way others see us. And by discarding what doesn't match up with our perceptions, we get stuck doing the same things over and over again—whether or not they get us any closer to our goal of meeting our soul mate.

Videos give you the opportunity to see what others do with new eyes; that is, they allow you to short-circuit the filters that your brain automatically uses to keep you focused on the things that match up with your idea of familiar. And the more you understand yourself, the more dating successes you'll have.

Of course, it's more than a bit daunting when you see yourself as others do and it's different from your self-concept. Coming to terms with this might be something you'll need to do before fully benefiting from the power of video. The danger? That you won't like what you see. And believe me, the fear of confronting your real self can be a huge obstacle to your progress.

But confront you must. Well, you must if you want to find the perfect partner. And that's what you're here for, right?

■ ■ ■

One day I accompanied Cara—a woman I was coaching—to a local Starbucks. There was great-looking guy in line whom she was attracted to and wanted to meet. So I said, "Go over there and smile at him."

Cara responded, "No. I go to this Starbucks all the time, and if I smile at him and he doesn't smile back, then I won't be able to come back here." The fear of potentially having to be reminded of a very public rejection—and the person who rejected her—each time she went to this particular place was strong enough to keep her from simply smiling at someone who might turn out to be Mr. Right.

Does this sound a little bit like you? Have you ever gone to the gym and really wanted to talk to somebody you were interested in and didn't? Do you understand why you passed up the opportunity? It's probably because you were afraid that if he or she rejected you, then you'd have to find a new gym. What about the grocery store? You would have to start shopping somewhere else. Or the elevator—what if you were rejected there? You'd have to move to a different apartment building.

This is just nuts.

This script in your head is just a made-up vision based in fear and insecurity—it's not real. Here's a news flash: except for maybe your mom and dad and your closest friends and family members, *nobody* cares about your life. The individuals you think are watching and judging you really aren't. And do you know why? It's because they're too busy criticizing their *own* lives. You see, they have the exact same issues as you do, the same misconceptions about themselves.

Maybe that girl you thought was cute at the park actually wanted to flirt with you, but she's also paralyzed by fear to do it because *she* doesn't want to deal with the possibility that she will be publicly humiliated when you reject her. Maybe the guy at the gym who you've been staring at for all this time wants to talk to you, but he's afraid that he'd be too embarrassed to go back if he approaches you and you don't show any interest.

Believe me, I hear these stories from my clients all the time, so I know that self-doubt constantly paralyzes so many of us—including those who seem beautiful, supremely confident, and infinitely secure on the surface.

Back in the mid-'90s, before I even started my business, I was watching Howard Stern's show on E!, and I remember that he said something really interesting. After being asked if he got hurt by all the people who say negative things about him, Howard responded in a way I'll never forget: "You know what? I don't care if people love me. I don't care if they hate me. As long as they're talking about me, that's all that matters. Because if they're talking about me, then I've created an emotion in them. And if I've created an emotion in them, it means that they actually are connecting to me, whether it's love or hate."

We all have fears and insecurities, and they do nothing at all to bring us closer to finding our perfect partner. In fact, they work overtime to keep us from doing just that. If we're to become datable, we've got to learn to let go of the things that are holding us back.

"Okay, fair enough," you might be saying. "But how exactly do I do that?"

Here's an example from my own life: I wasn't always the way I am, and I didn't always understand that I was the one who controlled the kind of man that other people saw. Part of the problem was that when I was growing up, the guidance I got from my dad wasn't always the best. When it came to giving me advice, he was very soft-spoken and noncommittal. But when it was time to criticize me, he was a different guy altogether. He put his heart into that task 110 percent.

Instead of helping to build my confidence, he would tear me down. Every single time I saw a girl and then looked at my feet, he'd say, "Why do you look at your feet? No son of mine should look at his feet. You're such a wimp with girls."

Instead of learning from him how to be self-assured with the opposite sex, I learned fear.

But even so, during my summer vacations, I was always able to do okay with girls. My father thought it would be good for me to experience something different every summer, so one year I was shipped off to a summer camp with a lake, cabins, and canoes, and the next year it was a tennis camp. But the year I did a summer teen tour was my favorite. It consisted of a bunch of spoiled kids who flew from New York to Denver, where we got on a bus (which we proceeded to ransack) and drove across the country, looking at inspiring national parks and monuments along the way. Actually, all we did was get on the bus, flirt, try to make out, and chew gum (which somehow always ended up stuck underneath our seats).

During these summers, I discovered that girls liked me because nobody knew who I was. Therefore, I was able to create a persona they found engaging. I got to be a totally different person—an actor trying out different roles. Once I figured that out, I made a point of being the most interesting, captivating guy possible. When I was at home, everyone knew me as David the shy guy.

I had a lot of friends and was reasonably popular, yet I was always very introverted with girls. But during summer vacations, watch out! I was a different kind of kid altogether—one who everyone wanted to meet.

My dad sent me away not because he wanted me to experience these things, but because he wanted to get rid of me for the summer. Regardless of his motivation, though, these times away from home were probably some of the best experiences of my childhood. They made me become more independent and taught me one of the greatest lessons of my entire life: when you go somewhere new, where no one knows you, you have a golden opportunity to re-create yourself as a superhero.

Admit it—you've thought about the fantastic, super-human version of yourself. What do you look like? Do you have a cape? Are you wearing cool little underwear? Are you a handsome but nerdy and shy guy like Clark Kent, who can transform into Superman when you see a damsel in distress? Or are you the dominatrix seductress dressed in tight black leather, like Catwoman?

I was able to totally revamp myself when I was a kid, and the same exact thing happened when I went to college. I was a complete stranger there, and therefore able to be an entirely new version of myself yet again. No one knew my fears. No one knew my insecurities. I wasn't the shy guy who was good with women one second and bad with them the next. Nobody knew that I was nervous and hesitant at times. People just saw whoever it was that I decided to be.

Because of these experiences, I've learned one of the most powerful coaching tools in my repertoire, which is taking a vacation in your own town. (You might remember it from Chapter 6.) For that one day, you create the persona that you've always wanted to be. You can be Joe Cool or Suzy Social. You're free to be the most interesting man or woman in the world, or you can fly under the radar. You can be the smart tech wizard or the disco-dancing star.

You can be anyone you want to be—including yourself, the *real* you. Try it sometime, it really works.

Fortunately, when I hit my 20s, I was able to get past the fear my dad had bestowed on me for years, and I didn't have to drag this baggage around with me any longer. But it wasn't easy, and it required a huge amount of self-awareness and the ability to see myself as others do. Once I understood that clearly, I realized what I needed to do. Video has the power to help you become self-aware, and then to comprehend what you need in order to change. And this knowledge makes all the difference in the world.

■ ■ ■

Unleashing the power of video requires an organized and sustained effort. Making a random movie isn't going to get you where you want to go. So the first thing I recommend you do—and this is really important—is to create a daily video journal. Every single day—rain or shine, good day or bad day—I want you to set aside some time to sit in front of a camera and talk. You can use a camcorder on a tripod, a webcam on your desktop, or a laptop computer to film yourself. If you're going to use a computer, there are plenty of free software programs available that enable you to create and edit video clips.

If you've seen the movie *Avatar,* you might remember that the human characters on the planet Pandora kept video journals. It was part of their routine, and it helped keep them grounded. I want you to do the same thing. Start each day by sitting in front of your camera and simply describe what's going on in your life.

Include things like:

- Where you're at in your dating life
- What you want in your dating life
- Who you are
- Who you're looking for
- What's important to you
- What you did (or will do) today to meet a potential partner
- What you did (or will do) today to become a more social person

Describe your life, talk about it, and store your videos somewhere so you can review them later. If you do that, you'll be able to look back a few weeks or months later and see how things have changed.

Next, I want you to start working on your voice tone. The energy behind what you say is extremely important when you approach someone you're interested in. It can be either an instant turn-on (or turn-off). I've found that reading a story—any story—is a great tool for working on your voice tone and energy. Just pick a few paragraphs to read from a book or magazine, and do so out loud while you're sitting in front of your camera. It doesn't matter what you decide to read, so long as it's something you're passionate about.

Pick up the sports section if that's what you enjoy, or a favorite short story. Or use an article about wine, food, or fashion if that's what inspires you. Now play back the video and focus on your voice. Are you clear and articulate, or do you come across as garbled and hard to understand? Are you full of energy and passion, or dull and lifeless? Do you speak with confidence, or are you tentative and shy? Your goal is to turn any of the negatives you see and hear into positives. So when you're doing something well, then do more of that. And when you're not, make a point of removing that aspect from your voice tone and replacing it with something more beneficial.

Keep practicing until you're consistently hitting the mark when it comes to the tone of your voice. Once you've gotten to that point, you'll know you're ready to take the next step.

■ ■ ■

Here's an exercise that I've found can work magic for building confidence and improving your approach: make a list of ten things you're passionate about, have stories about, and can easily discuss on camera. Once you have your list figured out, sit in front of your video camera and talk about each item. But don't just briefly mention them—I want you to describe each one with detail and passion. Bring yourself into the moment, like an actor does in a blockbuster Hollywood film. Once you're done, you should be able to tell ten exciting, interesting tales about your life.

For example, if you're a regular at Whole Foods, and you're passionate about the food they sell, then make that one of your topics. Personally, I know about almost all of the products at this store. I've tried, and love, the turkey meat loaf. So if I see someone eyeing it, I can look at her and say, "This is amazing—it's one of my favorites. It reminds me of how my grandmother used to make meat loaf."

Before I met my wife, I used to go out all the time for walks with my dog. And every time somebody saw me, they'd say, "God, your dog is so cute." They were right—she's a beautiful black English Lab.

I'd always ask in response, "Do you want her?" which would inevitably lead to an incredulous "Really?" from her admirer.

"Absolutely," I would say in return. "But she doesn't clean up after herself, and she won't get a job."

I told that same story over and over again, more times than I can even begin to remember. Why? Because I knew that it worked—I always got a laugh and a smile when I did so . . . and it even got me some dates as well. Stories are hooks. They're a way for people to quickly get an idea of what kind of person you are and gauge whether or not you're someone they'd like to get to know better. And it's far more exciting than talking about the weather.

You see, we literally repeat the same situations over and over again in our lives. We wait in line at the same bank, get coffee at the same Starbucks, grab lunch at the same deli around the corner from our office, take the same elevator at home and/or work, fill up our car at the same gas station, and go to the same dry cleaners on the corner. But within those seemingly mundane, day-to-day routines of life, there are things that we can be passionate about. And this passion can create great opportunities to communicate with someone we're interested in.

Now, if you find yourself going to the dry cleaners a lot, that means fashion and how you look are very important to you. If you're in your favorite coffee shop every day for your favorite whip cream–topped, caffeinated concoction, then you've probably got a real passion for coffee—how it's made, what part of the world the beans come from, and anything related to it. Or when you visit the mall and you frequent the same stores, chances are you really like their style and what they sell.

All these things are familiar to you and they have stories attached to them. So, what are you waiting for?

After you're done making the video—and this is the powerful part—review it and ask the following questions:

- Would *you* be interested in listening to yourself tell that story? Why or why not?

- Did you tell the story well?

- Did you drift off topic?

- How was your voice tone?

While you're watching, you can pause and practice adding in a new part that pops into your head. For example, you might say, "Oh my God, that's so cool. My grandmother made meat loaf the same way, and it was the best I've ever eaten." After you've worked your way through each topic—adding new parts as you go along—then repeat the cycle and record yourself again from the beginning. Repeat this process until you're totally satisfied with what you've created.

Can you see what I'm trying to do here? I'm attempting to make it so you'll always be completely present in the moment. This is because I truly believe that 99.9 percent of the best places to find dates are while you're doing what you do most often. There are an unlimited number of opportunities to meet potential mates every day.

The problem is that most of us are not great conversationalists—in fact, few people understand that the simple things in life are what we need to talk about. And I don't mean the weather; it's whatever we're passionate about.

So if you don't like your performance on film, go back and do it again.

Do it until you build up your confidence. Do it until you get your body language right. Do it until you smile. Do it over and over so you can learn how you convey your emotions to someone you're attracted to. Then take that knowledge and use it to improve your performance. Believe me. If rehearsing works for Brad Pitt or Angelina Jolie, then it can work for you, too.

■ ■ ■

The methods I've mentioned in this chapter are very powerful ways to use the magic of video to your advantage. However, there's an advanced technique that requires getting your friends involved, and it can take your efforts to a much higher level. If you would like to make the investment of your video time go even further, have a friend follow you around with your camcorder so you'll be able to see for yourself just how you act in your everyday life.

To get started on this exercise, write down the number of individuals you think noticed you today. Most people will say zero, because they're so preoccupied with their phones and just getting from one place to another as quickly as possible.

Now, here's where you're going to be surprised by what you wrote down. If you have a friend follow you around and record you while you're in public, it's amazing what you'll see. You'll immediately notice opportunities for social contact everywhere you go. You're going to see people smile at you, watch you as you walk down the aisle in the supermarket, and check you out as you pass them. The reason you haven't realized that this was happening before is because very few individuals really pay attention to everything that's going on around them. The average person is lost in his or her thoughts or focused on daily goals, totally oblivious to the immediate environment.

And we literally miss out on hundreds of chances to meet the man or woman who's going to make a real difference in our lives for years to come.

Once you've written down how many people you think noticed you today, get a friend to film you for at least a half hour. Go to a grocery store or a mall, or just walk down a busy street. This person shouldn't be worried about sticking out in the crowd with the camera. (Now that recording devices have shrunk down to the size of a deck of cards, it's really no big deal. Most cell phones nowadays even have video capabilities built into them, and they're even less obtrusive.)

After the recording session, go home and watch the results. What do you see? I can guarantee that you'll notice far more heads turning to notice you than you ever imagined, checking you out and even trying to catch *your* attention.

Do you know why? Because they're interested in you.

To meet the people you want to meet, you have to learn to pay attention to everything that's going on around you 24/7 while you're out in public. In each of these social situations, you need to be very aware of your body language. Is it inviting to others, or does it shout "I'm too busy for you—stay away!" Not only that, but you also need to develop your own observation skills. Are you constantly scanning your surroundings as you walk, or do you only look straight ahead like a horse with blinders on? Be mindful of how you walk. Do you walk so fast that you miss the obvious moments to make an impression on those around you, or do you make an entrance in such a way that people notice you?

This approach of leveraging the power of video is particularly useful because it enables you to learn how to present yourself with confidence and awareness in any situation. I use these methods with my clients, and they really work—they're some of the most effective self-awareness exercises you can do. It's no secret why professional athletes, actors, dancers, or any performers are constantly watch videos of themselves. They can instantly see what they did right, what they did wrong, and how they can do it better the next time.

■ ■ ■

In the next chapter, we're going to put some of the lessons you've learned from this chapter to work. We'll explore how you can build your own brand. If it can work for Procter & Gamble, Coca-Cola, and Southwest Airlines (and believe me, it does), then it can also work for you.

■ ■ ■

CHAPTER 13

BUILD BRAND YOU

How many times have you gone into a store to buy something—say, a bottle of shampoo or some toothpaste—and you immediately reach for a particular brand without even looking at any others? Even though competitors' products may be just as good or even better, you're more attracted to the one you always use and no other. It just has a certain appeal to you, and you feel good buying it.

That's the power of a brand.

Marketers know that our brains are more attracted to certain products over others, and that this attraction can be manipulated. Businesses, advertisers, sports teams, the government—everybody—spend a fortune on branding their products and building an identity for themselves. The Dallas Cowboys are called America's Team. M&M's melt in your mouth, not in your hand. Miller Lite beer tastes great and is less filling. And then there's Allstate. Are you in good hands?

But while organizations of all kinds spend tons of money coming up with their unique identities, few people spend any time at all creating their own personal brand, and this is a mistake.

Whenever a client works with me, one of the first things I do is help them with their personal brand—who they are, what they stand for, and how they want the world to see them. When you walk into a room, you want to make a statement. But what do you want to say? Your hairstyle, your clothing, the way you walk, and the way you talk are essential elements in your personal brand, which broadcasts the kind of person you are to everyone you interact with.

My private weekends start at $9,000. I know some of you gasped just now and said to yourself, *I don't believe it!* Well, it's true. And the reason I can command that kind of fee for a weekend of my time is because I have created my own coaching brand—the David Wygant brand—and people are convinced that what I sell will deliver the satisfaction they're looking for. When they buy my brand, they know they're going to get value from their work with me. That's what this is all about.

When you meet someone for the very first time— say, in a bar or at the dog park—the person wants to know that he or she is going to get value from *you*. They want to have no doubt that for the time and energy they invest in you, they're going to get someone who is confident, secure, funny, quirky, athletic, smart, or whatever your brand is.

I recently did a private weekend workshop with a client named Robert. The first thing I noticed was that he was dressed and behaved just like his dad (based on the photo he showed me of them together at a Texas Rangers baseball game and what he told me). So I assumed that he wanted to be like his father. He also told me that his dad was conservative, yet Robert was trying to stay away from that classification. Additionally, he didn't want to look like a nerd from the suburbs—he desired to be hip and cool, and to give off the appearance of someone who lived in the city. He wanted women to look at him and think to themselves, *That guy is cool.* But to achieve this goal, my client needed to change his product packaging. And not only did he need a new wrapper—an entirely new set of clothes that weren't 20 years out of date—he needed an entirely new attitude. The logic behind this is if you look good, you'll feel better about yourself, and therefore, you'll exude confidence and power.

Companies spend countless hours and dollars developing the packaging for their products. Coca-Cola has tried all sorts of new can designs, but keep coming back to the same one that they've used for decades, because that's what resonates with their customers. Starbucks recently went back to one of their older logos, since they found that people thought of the brand in a more favorable light when they saw it.

So, given that companies dedicate so much time and money to their brands, why do so many individuals spend such a small amount of their resources on their own brands?

■ ■ ■

I see all sorts of people being cheap with their personal identity . . . and men are especially guilty in this area. When most guys go shopping, they don't think about what they're projecting when they buy a shirt. They wonder how many years they'll get out of it. They want to get every dollar's worth out their clothes.

I went through a male client's closet one time, and I was surprised—but not shocked—by what I saw. My client's wardrobe looked like it was straight out of the 1980s. I asked him, "Is this your personal brand—high-waisted jeans and shirts that haven't been in style for decades? Do you really want people to think that you have no fashion sense at all, that you're someone who doesn't care about the way he looks? Is that the way you want the world to see you?"

He decided that it was time to update his look, so we made a beeline to Nordstrom, and we shopped. And we shopped. And we shopped some more. It was hard for my client at first. He didn't have any problem putting down $2,000 for a business suit, because he wanted people to know he was successful. But when it came to his personal wardrobe, he was a cheapskate.

It's funny how people will spend a lot of money on their professional branding when they're buying their work clothes. They want to be seen as successful, because they know that clients and customers want to do business with those who exude success. After all, this means money in the bank. They also know that if they don't dress their best, this could ultimately mean a loss of profits. But while they're willing to spend money on building their professional persona, they're not willing to invest in their own personal brand.

Hello! It's the same thing!

If you want to be successful with the opposite sex, you've got to dress the part. And this starts by figuring out what your personal brand is, and then buying the clothes that project it. Do you want to be the cool athletic type; the dressy, chic sophisticate; or maybe the studied, casual preppy? Whatever you decide on, it has to reflect exactly who *you* are. You've got to feel great about yourself. This is all about how you want people to see you when you walk into a room. It's your packaging. And even though we've been working on your inner packaging throughout this book, we can't forget about the outer packaging—it's really important, too!

■ ■ ■

As for me, I know myself well—I'm cool, I'm hip, I'm trendy yet classic. I'm someone who cares about my appearance, but who feels more comfortable in jeans than a suit. So my power suit is a great pair of jeans, a stylish shirt, and a cool pair of boots. That's my personal brand on the outside.

On the inside, I'm strong, powerful, and confident. I go after what I desire—I don't hesitate. When you're in my presence, you're with somebody who knows what he wants. I speak my mind at all times, which may or may not work with certain individuals, but that's me. I'm all about revealing my truth and not hiding behind false words. I also listen very closely to what others say, because part of my identity is really connecting with people. I want everyone to feel at home, safe, and secure when they're around me.

Those are some things that make my personal brand what it is.

Now it's time for another exercise. I want you to write down answers to the following questions:

- What is your personal brand?

- What does it stand for?

- If you had to write a personal brand statement about who you are, what would it be? (This should only be about two to three sentences in length.)

Next, take a look through your closet and ask yourself if your clothes match what you just wrote. Just as brands need freshening up every few years, have you updated your wardrobe lately? If you can't remember when you bought the items in your closet, then you're past due for a makeover.

If you're not sure what to buy or where to start, go to the mall and do some observing. Whenever you see someone who is dressed in a way you like—and that you think reflects brand you—then make a note of what the person is wearing. What kind of shirt does he or she have on? What kind of blouse, pants, dress, or skirt? Shoes? Boots? Jacket? Tie? What about the fabrics, colors, and styles? Take it all in. Look at people who you think look really cool and have the same body type, height, and age range as you. When you see individuals with great outfits on, go up and ask them where they bought them.

Once you get some new ideas for your wardrobe, do some shopping with a focus on reinventing your personal brand. Try stuff on and ask others around you if they like the way things fit. Coincidentally, this is also a great way to meet people. As you're out there working on your personal brand, you have a golden opportunity to meet potential mates as you interact with them and ask what they think about what you're trying on. It's a great way to expand your social network and get dates.

Finally, take pictures of yourself. Post some of them on Facebook, and send them to friends, asking, "What do you think of this?" or "If you had to put a caption underneath the photo, what would it be?"

Creating brand you is a lot of fun. Just keep in mind that it's a process that involves who you are on both the inside *and* the outside. You can't skimp or be cheap about anything, because potential mates will only see what they want to see.

In the next chapter we'll consider why it's never a good idea to try to change the person you're in a relationship with—even if that change is for the better.

■ ■ ■

CHAPTER 14

STOP TRYING TO CHANGE PEOPLE

I write a new blog post every day on my website. After one particular post, readers made a crazy amount of comments—about 200 or so. The heated response I received is what inspired me to include this chapter.

Are you somebody who is a *change agent*, someone who likes to rescue others? If so, what's the deal? People are who they are. A personal pet peeve of mine is when individuals date someone based on potential. They'll say, "Wow, I love this person so much! He's [she's] awesome. He's [she's] got so much potential."

Really? I used to hear that all the time when I was in school. Starting in third grade, my parents would go to parent-teacher night. And then they would come home and always say the same thing: "David, your English teacher thinks you're the best writer in class. If you could just learn grammar—you have so much potential to be a great writer, a fantastic writer." So I thought to myself, *I'm a fantastic writer now. But now you're telling me that all I need to do is learn grammar? Isn't there someone who can edit my work?*

I remember going back to school the next day and talking to my English teacher. She looked at me and she said, "Your parents were so nice. We discussed how great your writing is."

"Yes, I know. I have a lot of potential."

"Yes, you do," she responded. "But you need to focus more."

I looked her square in the eye and replied, "I want to ask you a question. My writing is really fun, right?"

"Oh, it's the best! It's the most entertaining writing in the class, and it's very powerful."

"Well, if it's so great, let me just continue writing great stuff, and quit trying to change me."

Here's the deal: You can't change people. If you're with someone who's not right for you, or has behavior patterns that you can't accept, you're wasting your time if you think you can change him or her. You're not a change agent.

A lot of women will date men who are emotionally immature, and then they're surprised when the relationship isn't what they wanted it to be. But they'll go out with these childish guys again and again. Remember the definition of insanity from Chapter 4? It's doing the same thing over and over and expecting a different result.

■ ■ ■

Here's a note that I received from a woman who continued to make the same decisions and expected a different result:

> David, I want to tell you about a bad relationship
> that I went through some time ago. I knew that this

guy wasn't exactly right for me, but he kept talking about how he was changing his life, and he appeared to be heading in the right direction. He just needed a little bit of help. But before I knew it, he sucked the life right out of me. Everything was always about him. His self-centered behavior not only destroyed our relationship, but it also damaged many of my other relationships—personally and professionally. Unfortunately, at the time I was young, I was dumb, and I really thought I could change him. I believed in the potential I saw in this man, and I put all my energy into him. In return for my faith, he proceeded to trash me emotionally, mentally, and financially. I should have said, "Enough!" but I couldn't because I was so vested in the process of improving him. I couldn't let go of my vision of how great I thought he could be once I was able to "fix" him. Eventually, I lost any trace of respect for this guy. I grew to resent him, and I finally gave in and ended things.

What a waste of this woman's precious time and energy! The truth of the matter is that so many of you are involved with partners who are emotionally challenged, unbalanced, and immature. A lot of you look at the potential of your prospective mates and are blind to the reality that you can't change people, and it's a waste of your time to try and rescue them. By doing so, *you* become the victim. You get sucked into this person's world, he or she takes all your energy, and the relationship becomes toxic.

You can't rescue others; they need to do that themselves. They must look at themselves in the mirror and realize that whatever selfish behavior patterns they have are destroying every relationship they ever had in the past and will have in the future. It's not up to you to teach them that lesson. It's not on you to show them how life can really be. Instead of wasting your time with those whom you feel you need to change, why not get into a dating situation where the other person is someone who's already right for you?

■ ■ ■

I have a client who's notorious for trying to "help" the women he dates. He'll go out with a woman and then say, "God, she's absolutely beautiful! But if she'd just lose 15 pounds, she'd be perfect. I'm going to buy her a gym membership and hire her a personal trainer."

What about the beautiful person that she is *now?* Maybe she'll never lose the weight, and most likely she'll come to resent this guy for always trying to change her.

Stop looking at the potential of your mates, and stop trying to be such a change agent. Look at them for who they are right now. Are you into certain individuals exactly the way they are right now—not the ways you think you can change them, how you think you can mold their lives, or to make them what you want them to be? Are you willing to accept them 100 percent the way they are—including their extra pounds, their love of prime-time television, their lack of motivation, or whatever it might be?

■ ■ ■

It's time for an exercise. Look at all the relationships that you've had and ask yourself, *How many times and how many years have I spent trying to be a change agent for someone? How many times have I tried to fix or rescue the people I care about, and how did it impact my life?*

Then I want you to look at your present dating situation and consider whether or not this behavior is going to satisfy you. If you're completely honest with yourself, I think you'll realize that you can't be satisfied. People don't change unless they make the decision to do so themselves.

■ ■ ■

You have only one chance to make a first impression, so make it the very best one you possibly can. This is true not only at the beginning of a date, but also when you "meet" someone via an online-dating website. In the next chapter, we'll consider some of the promises and pitfalls of the online-dating experience, and how to make it a positive one for you and your prospective dates.

■ ■ ■

CHAPTER 15

NAVIGATE THE ONLINE-DATING WORLD

In today's electronically enabled online world, you no longer have to stand in a bar, buy five drinks, and put up with smoke being blown in your face in order to get a date. (Then again, many cities have actually banned cigarettes in bars and restaurants.)

As a side note, I worked in bars for a long time when I lived in New York City. At the end of my shift, I would come home after talking to and serving people all night—entertaining them, pushing alcohol on them, and getting them inebriated so they would think they had a good time . . . and hopefully come back the very next day and do the same thing all over again. I remember breathing in that smoke and realizing that it was killing me little by little. If you're a smoker, that's fine—that's your business. But I personally can't stand cigarettes.

Anyway, one of the great things about dating today is that you don't even need to be near people, let alone hang out in a bar, get drunk, and wake up the next day with a hangover. You can literally sit at home day or night and shop for men or women. I call it "**manazon .com**" and "**womanazon.com.**" You can spend hours cruising profiles, reading about people and their dreams and aspirations, their likes and dislikes. And let me tell you, online-dating profiles are some of the best fiction reading I have ever seen in my entire life.

It's amazing how everybody is fit and slim, down-to-earth, and honest in this cyberworld. During coaching sessions, one of the things I do with men who are inexperienced and haven't dated a lot is tell them that their goal should be to learn about women. One of the best ways to do so is to go to one of these websites—**match .com** or **okcupid.com**, for example—join for a month, and just read women's profiles. My clients learn so much about potential girlfriends that way, including how they think, their wishes, and their desires.

By doing this yourself, you'll figure out the ones who are more sexually promiscuous—the ones who tip you off in their profile that they might be ready to have a little bit of fun. You'll learn about the ones who have been hurt before, and also get a pretty good sense of how they were hurt and their desire to avoid going down that path again. You'll encounter "listers," the women that make a to-do list every day, or maybe even highlight things in different colors in their Day-Timer.

And, of course, if you're a woman, you can do the same thing by reading men's profiles. You'll find out so much about the opposite sex from these sites, without even meeting anyone in person.

When the men I coach have pursued this exercise for a month, they've come back and told me, "Okay, now I've got a general idea of what women are all about. The more profiles I read, the easier it was for me to relate to females." This is because they were starting to understand women's emotional core.

I always say that women speak in emotions, and there are always two different stories to everything. To give you an example, here's the same story told twice, first by a man and then by a woman.

A guy went to Italy on vacation, and afterward he sits down with his friend and says, "I had a great time in Italy—it's a beautiful country. Now, what do you want to eat?"

A woman, however, will take an entirely different approach to the same conversation:

"I had this amazing adventure in Italy!"

"Tell me more," her friend urges.

"Oh my god, you wouldn't believe it! I was wine tasting at a vineyard in the Italian countryside, and there was, like, this really hot guy there. I thought he was Italian, until he walked over and said hi. With a *Texan* accent, he asked, 'Are you American?' And then he smiled. And I was thinking to myself, *I can't believe I've got to go all the way to Italy to meet a hot guy from Texas!*"

That's how women tell stories—they tell *emotions*.

Anyway, a lot of people start off their online-dating experience in the wrong way. They put a profile up before they've done some simple market research.

Think about it for minute. If you run a business, you need to know what your customer wants, right? You need to know what he or she is looking for. So what do you do? You do a little bit of market research by asking your customers questions and finding out more about their needs and desires. But you don't make major changes in your products or services until you first find out what people are looking for.

In online dating, people regularly put profiles of themselves up without looking at the competition or understanding the wants and desires of their "customers." They don't even read about their prospective mates. They just post information and wait for the offers to flood in. And then they're surprised when they get little or no response.

Don't you think that before you put your profile up, you should see what the competition is writing in order to get an idea of how they're presenting themselves? As you research, ask yourself this question: *Would I be interested in this person?* Whether you're reading about a male or female doesn't make a difference, because you're learning to navigate the world of online dating and make yourself stand out.

After you've looked through a few profiles, then spend some serious time studying your target market. If you're interested in men between the ages of 25 and 35, then do a search in that age range and check out those profiles. If you're after brunette women with college educations between the ages of 40 and 45, then enter those characteristics into the search fields and read as many of them as you can.

■ ■ ■

Getting to know potential mates online is an entirely different experience from getting to know them in person. As far as I'm concerned, it's a singles bar in the sky. There are people there sucking down cocktails and having little parties in front of their computers. Go on **Match.com** on a Friday night at 10:00 and see if I'm right. Sign in and send somebody you're interested in a quick message—something cute and clever like, "What are *you* doing home tonight? Are you man-shopping [or woman-shopping]?" You'll probably get a flirtatious response right back, and possibly even the promise of an in-person date.

And that's what makes a well-timed e-mail such an effective tool—you're calling people out on the obvious. What do you *think* they're doing at 10:00 on a Friday night? Of course, they're shopping for love. They went out to a bar or club, had a glass of wine, didn't like what they saw, and went home and decided to go online and do some man- or woman-shopping.

Here's where I'm going with this: Everybody online creates fantasy versions of themselves. People say they're 39 even though they're 46. They're fit and trim—"athletic"—even though they're 30 or 40 pounds overweight and haven't seen the inside of a gym since they were in high school. They're adventurous, even though their idea of an adventure is taking a trip to the grocery store. They're down-to-earth, which just means that they don't complain as much as their brothers or sisters. And they're spontaneous and living in the moment, yet they can't survive without their daily to-do lists.

Online dating is a contradiction inside a conundrum. When you're seeking a mate via the Internet, what you're really doing is trying to sort through all the profiles (essentially, product advertisements) and find the real gems. And they *are* out there—more and more people are using online dating sites to do their mate shopping. But finding successful relationships using this method requires a lot of truth and honesty from all sides.

You need to first be honest with yourself. Your profile should be real, not the souped-up version of yourself. This means describing the things you *really* like to do—like sitting around watching TV every night with your cat in your lap instead of making up something about how you regularly jump out of airplanes or climb mountains—even if you don't think they're what will attract the best mate. Write down who you are and what you're really all about.

When you're genuine about who you are, someone who has similar values (your perfect mate?) will have the best chance of finding, and being completely happy with, the *real* you. And that's ultimately who you want to be with—someone whose path resembles yours. After you meet, you can learn and grow and teach each other new things.

Here's a tip—no, here's a *commandment.* Let other people lie. Let other people put up ten-year-old pictures of when they had fewer wrinkles, weren't 25 pounds overweight, and had some hair left on their heads. Let them create fake versions of themselves. What you're looking for is a gem—a real person who shares the same needs and desires as you do. Instead of measuring your success in the world of online dating by the *quantity* of dates you get, measure it by the *quality* of the dates you get. This means taking the time to search for the treasures, and quickly discarding the phonies.

■ ■ ■

I have another exercise for you. This one will help you locate the gems and filter out the individuals who will simply waste your time and energy.

First, read some profiles of your competition—people of the same sex (assuming you're looking for someone of the opposite sex). Note the kinds of things that they're offering their prospective "customers" and the way they say it. Can you sense when someone is boasting, showing off, or being fake? Do you feel sincerity, honesty, and quiet self-confidence in their words? How are these emotions expressed, and what lessons can you learn for writing your own profile?

Second, read lots of profiles of your target market—people who are in the age range you're interested in and share the same basic likes and dislikes. Be aware of exactly what kind of mates they're looking for and how they express this. What lessons can you learn and apply to your own profile?

Third, create your profile. Be sure to write about who you really are—sharing interesting insights about yourself and the kind of person you're looking for. Be cool about it. For example, you're looking for someone who's seeking adventure; someone who can share what his or her life has been about; someone who really wants to grow and learn and do things they never have before; someone who will be a partner and a best friend; or someone who's emotionally, mentally, and physically ready to experience the best life has to offer.

Above all, be positive when you fill out your profile. No one wants to bring a negative person into his or her life.

After you're done, read it out loud—especially the part that describes who you are. Is this anyone you'd like to meet? Does he or she resonate with you? Is the profile written with confidence? If the answer to any of these questions is no, then you've got some work to do before you go live with it on the dating site.

If you're not happy with your profile, take another look at other people's—men or women—and closely observe how they speak about themselves. Ask friends of both sexes to read your profile and give you feedback on how to improve it. Have them tell you if it really sounds like you or if you're embellishing.

You need to be truthful. If you lie on your online profile—whether it's with words, your age, or photos—your date is going to feel let down when the individual he or she read about doesn't show up when you meet in person. And if you don't live up to your advertising, then you're bound to have a very disappointing night. You just wasted someone's time, and you wasted your own time. The longer you're dishonest about your profile, the longer you're going to continue to have a lot of one-and-done dates with people you don't resonate with.

I'd rather go out with ten women I was being honest and accurate with than 100 who were disappointed when I arrived. Believe me, lying in life will never get you anywhere good, and that's definitely true when it comes to online dating.

And guess what, when you're truthful about who you are, you'll stand out in a sea of fakes and wannabes.

■ ■ ■

Every great endeavor needs a great plan to guide it, and this is undoubtedly true when it comes to dating. In the next chapter, we'll explore how to create a plan for your life. In doing so, you'll learn the secret to unlocking your deepest feelings, dreams, and emotions; and how to begin the process of accepting who you really are. Doing this will put you well on your way to attracting and meeting your perfect match.

■ ■ ■

CHAPTER 16

PLAN FOR LIFE

Do you look at your life as a marathon or a sprint? Do you compare yourself to other people and think, *I'm never going to get there?* Are you in a situation where having a family has eluded you, and you feel like you'll never accomplish your dream of being happily married with kids, living in a beautiful house with that white picket fence?

Who says you're too old to do any of that stuff? No matter what your age might be, you're never too old to start living your dreams.

I was recently talking to a client who is 41 and very frustrated with his life. As he explained, "I don't like my career and would like to make a change. But I'm afraid that if I go through with it and it doesn't work out, I'm not going to be able to get anywhere . . . it's going to be all over for me."

This guy had already been married—and divorced—once, and he wanted to have children. But he felt that at the ripe old age of 41, it was too late for any of that. Even worse, he was convinced that if he couldn't make his dream happen within the next week, it would just pass him by.

But guess what? Life doesn't work that way. You can have whatever you want at whatever age you want it. Ultimately, it's you who decides what path to take, and it's you who defines success on your own terms. If you see yourself as a complete and utter failure, then you've just created a self-fulfilling prophecy. Because you visualize your life in terms of failure instead of success, you're going to create negative energy all around you. You'll have a doomsday attitude of not being able to get anywhere in life.

The people you meet every day will notice this behavior and either be repelled by it or attracted to it. And guess who's going to be attracted to that kind of outlook? That's right, the individuals who themselves visualize their own lives in terms of failure instead of success. These are certainly not the types of personalities you want or need in your life.

Listen up: life is all about how you look at things, and by having a positive mind-set, you can create the kind of life you want and deserve.

But first you need a plan.

Life is a marathon, not a sprint. And if we look at it as such, it means that eventually we're going to get to where we want to go. Sure, some of us reach our goals at a young age—maybe right out of high school or college. We find the person we're going to spend the rest of our lives with, we find the career we're supposed to be in, and we start a family and are content with who we've become. However, some of us may be 40, 50, or even 60 years of age before we fulfill our ambitions. Sadly, some of us don't get there at all.

Which camp are you in? Because you're reading this chapter, I'm going to guess that you haven't yet found the satisfaction you're looking for. This puts you squarely in the latter camp. Or maybe you've had great moments or years, but you desire consistency.

How much of your life has worked out exactly the way you planned? Have you ever gone home for the holidays and had your mother ask, while looking you dead in the eye, "What's wrong with you? Why haven't you met a great man [woman] yet? I don't understand."

When I tell older people what I do for a living, they always want to tell me about their kids. You know parents—they want their sons and daughters to have the same opportunities in life that they had, and that most often means being married and having kids. So a lot of moms and dads can't handle it when they discover that their children actually want something different. I can remember one time I was talking to a woman on an American Airlines flight. She was absolutely convinced that there was something wrong with her son. He had a very successful job as an accomplished graphic designer at a thriving business; however, he was an utter failure (as far as his mother was concerned) when it came to relationships. He was 31 years old, unmarried, and without children. Mom just *knew* something was wrong with her son, and she wanted me to give her some advice on how to "fix" him.

I asked, "Do you know if he even wants kids?"

She looked at me sternly and replied, *"Everybody* wants kids."

"That's not true. There are a lot of people out there who just want to live their own lives, travel, or not be responsible for another human being. Have you ever just sat down with your son and asked him exactly what he wants in life?"

"No," she answered. "I just assumed he wanted what I had."

That's what a lot of parents do—they assume that their kids want exactly what they have. And they also want grandchildren to visit, family dinners, and holiday parties. And if their kids are getting to a certain age, and they aren't married and having kids of their own, then there must be something wrong with them—right?

Wrong!

If you're single and your parents are always trying to push you to get married, I want you to do this exercise: Tomorrow, call or visit them and explain exactly what it is you're looking for in life. By doing this, you've got a fighting chance to provide them with a vision of your dreams that matches your own. If you're happily single and looking forward to a kid-free lifestyle, then explain that to them. If you're planning to hold off for another five or ten years before you start getting serious about finding a long-term partner and settling down, then tell them that, too. Just be honest, and speak from your heart. If you do this, then maybe—just maybe—your mother or father won't sit down next to me on the next American Airlines flight from Los Angeles to New York City and complain about you for two hours while I'm trying to read a book.

■ ■ ■

Most people have a *dream plan*, but what is missing from their "Martin Luther King, Jr., moment" is an *action plan*. Yes, Dr. King had a dream, but he also had a plan to put it into action—step-by-step, day by day.

For you sports fans, let me explain it this way. Consider a football player who has recently been drafted into the NFL. He'll have to go through many trials and tribulations to realize his goals of becoming one of the game's greats. This means practicing every single day, throwing the ball, rushing, and tackling. A good player has to first master the fundamentals if he ever hopes to become great.

This is true for all of us, no matter what our goals may be. To become successful, we have to first master the basics, because the big things in life are a series of fundamentals done the right way.

When I was 24 years old, I was frustrated and wanted a career. My friend Howard told me, "David, I know you want a career. I also know you want to meet a great woman one day. I know you want all this stuff, but you've got to master the small things first. You've got to become good and do the best job that you can at whatever you're doing, in whatever stage you're at, because that's the only way you're ever going to achieve your goals and dreams."

Howard was right on target. From that point on, I became very focused on being the best I possibly could at everything I did. You've got to realize that you're where you're supposed to be in your life right now. You may be alone, you may be single, and you're either loving or hating it. But regardless of your situation and your feelings about it, this is where you are. You can't reflect on your failed relationships and think about what could've and should've been. The only thing you can look at is the present.

You can't change the past, but you *can* choose to do something different in the present. Starting today, you can focus on getting better at meeting people so you'll be able to find the love you've been dreaming about. You can decide that you won't rest until you find your truth—exactly who you want to be. You are where you are personally and professionally because of the choices you've made. And you made them because they're part of your journey. Without these choices, your journey could not, and would not, exist.

So if you feel as if your life is over or you're frustrated because you're not where you want to be yet, you've got to get down to basics.

■ ■ ■

Here's an exercise you can do right now to help. Write down all your dreams, in detail. Where do you want to be, and what do you want your life to look like tomorrow? Six months from now? A year from now? Five years from now? How do you want to feel? Where do you want to travel? What kind of car do you want to drive? What type of house do you want to live in? What job do you want? Don't leave anything out.

Everybody has a right to dream, but without taking action, nothing will never happen. I know because I live in Los Angeles, a city that's full of dreamers. Everybody you meet here has a grand vision. There's the financial planner who'd rather be playing a financial planner on television. Then there's that cop who pulled you over for running the stop sign—he hoped you were a producer, because he's got a script that he wants to sell you. And there's the waitress serving you dinner who thinks that her work is really beneath her. In her mind, she's actually the most talented actress in the world, since that's what all her friends (who are all also dreamers) tell her.

But, in reality, that waitress should realize that she's got to give you the best possible service and have the most amount of fun she can, since by doing so she's going to attract the right kind of people into her life. Instead, she's repelling them. As I said earlier in the book, life is a stage. Everything you do presents you with an opportunity to attract—or repel—somebody else.

So as you're writing down all of your dreams, remember that you've got to act in order to make them happen. So if you want to live in a big house in ten years, what are the actions you've got to take today in order to make that happen? You can't just wave your arms and do some hoodoo-voodoo stuff to instantly manifest a beautiful home just because you're a good person.

We *all* deserve a big house because we're good people, right? But that doesn't mean that we're all going to be able to afford one.

What actions are you going to take to achieve your dreams? This is a key point—so much so that when you put your dreams to paper, make sure you write down the steps you're going to take in order to make them come true. If you want to meet a fantastic girl or guy and go out on ten dates per month, for example, and right now you're only going out on one every other month, how are you going to get to your magic number of ten? Well, you're going to need to start talking to more potential mates for one thing.

So, how many new people are you going to talk to every single day to accomplish this goal? How are you going to build your social skills to make it easier to meet these new individuals? What are your conversational skills like right now? Are you good at meeting strangers or not? How are you going to learn how to become the most powerful social version of yourself?

The actions that will enable you to become the most powerful social version of yourself are exactly what are needed for you to be able to attain your dreams.

Now, let's say you want to have a great car—what job are you going to find to enable you to save enough money or make the monthly payments to afford it? How are you going to manage your finances differently than you do right now? What are you going to eliminate in your life in order to save up for the down payment?

Or what if you want to lose weight—what steps are you going to take to make this happen? Are you going to just talk about getting back into shape like so many "dieters"? People try to talk themselves back into shape all the time. They say, "I've got to get back into shape," "I'm going to hit the gym next week," or "I'm going to start that diet next week." Then when you see them three weeks later and ask how their diet or gym program is going, they'll say, "I haven't done it yet, but I'm going to soon."

Guess what? Talking yourself into shape doesn't work. Regardless, I know plenty of people who try to do so over and over again. If getting fit is one of your goals, here's how you can really do it. Go to the gym one day the first week. The following week, go twice, picking whatever day you'd like. Then the following week, go three days. When you work yourself up to four days a week, all of a sudden you'll start shedding the pounds. There's no miracle cure or diet, just as there are no miraculous ways to make money or meet your soul mate. No matter what your mantra is, and no matter what you tell yourself, there are no miracles here. Just hard work.

And the problem with this is that so many people don't want to do what it takes, because that means having to do things differently. If you want to make lasting changes in your life, you'll need to practice doing them every day for 30 days. At the end of that time, you'll have developed a new habit.

I remember being 19 years old when I first started working out. I was quite skinny, and I always looked at bigger guys and wanted to be like them. So I talked my way into shape. I would say over and over again, "I'm going to get big one day. I'm going to start working out and lifting weights.

Actually, I had weights in my house, but I never used them.

Then one day—true story—the movie *Flashdance* came out, and I watched people getting really physical. There was just something about it. I know it's nothing that the average guy would watch to get motivated for a work out, but I went home and lifted weights that same night.

But I didn't see any miracles happen right away . . . after all, that's what we're all looking for, right? So if you're a little thick in the stomach and you want to tighten it up, you might do 100 sit-ups. Then you look in the mirror, and your stomach looks exactly the same. In reality, what happens is that deep down things are starting to change, all because of that little bit of work you did.

So I did it. I stopped talking and started doing. And it worked—I started to shape up and get healthy.

Similarly, I remember in my 20s when I wanted to be really smooth with women. What did I do every single day? I walked around New York City and forced myself to communicate with people based on natural observations. As a result, I became a good conversationalist. And little by little, I got better. Yes, I was frustrated at times. Yes, I had times when I was pissed off. Yes, I had setbacks. But I did it.

Then, when I built a business, I took steps every single day toward my goal. Did I want to make money? Absolutely. But in the beginning, the cash wasn't rolling in. I had to build the foundation, and I did that by taking action and working 14- to 17-hour days to make the company successful. If you want something bad enough, you've got to do whatever it takes to make it happen.

Every day builds a foundation. Step-by-step, you'll get there. You just have to be willing to do the difficult tasks. You have to be willing to fail. You have to be willing to pick yourself up each day and embrace the small victories. Life is not just talking the talk—you've got to walk the walk, too.

If you're more of a dreamer than a doer, you might find this to be a huge challenge. So if you find the action part to be really tough, then I suggest you read this chapter at least six to ten times. The more you do, the more you're going to realize and admit to yourself that this is where you need the most amount of work. If this is the one chapter in the book that really resonates deeply within you, work on it. You can go back to the rest whenever you want. But it's vital for you to understand that you are the only one who can realize his or her dreams. You're the only one who's responsible for your success, your happiness, and everything else that you want in life.

In the next chapter, we'll discuss why it's important for you create your own rule book and then live by it.

■ ▉ ■

CHAPTER 17

LIVE YOUR RULE BOOK

What I am about to tell you might make you feel like putting up your dukes. I'm going to challenge the way you live your life.

Are you—right now—living a life completely by your own rules? I'm not talking about your parents' rules, your boss's rules, or your partner's rules. Living your life by other people's rules—no matter how well-intentioned they may be—means that you're living their lives, dreams, frustrations, and visions for you.

A few years ago, I was hanging out with a client named Sharon, and she was telling me how she lived according to her father's rules. She was supposed to date a certain type of man: a nice Jewish boy from the suburbs; after all, she was a nice Jewish girl from the suburbs. But there was a problem—Sharon wasn't attracted to the nice Jewish boys from the suburbs. That was her father's vision for her, not her own. So every time Sharon dated outside the suburban Jewish community, her father would say, "Really? That's who you're dating? I didn't bring you up like that. That's not who you're supposed to be with!"

Have you ever gotten that kind of message from family members, friends, or others? I'm going to guess that you've heard plenty of similar comments in your own life. People try to get you to live according to their rules, and the temptation to give in can be hard to resist. You see, the fear of being the last single person standing can be a very powerful motivator. If all of your friends are married or in loving relationships, you'll feel pressure to find someone yourself. Certain individuals become so influenced by their friends that they end up jumping into situations that they should have avoided or missing out on mates who would have been a perfect match.

All because they're not living their lives according to their own rule book.

■ ■ ■

There was this woman I met at Whole Foods a long time ago, and we ended up having a great connection and conversation. I was jazzed about it. Everything seemed as if it was exactly the way it should have been—it was one of those serendipitous moments that we're all looking for, where meeting someone new feels natural and real. I then did exactly what I was supposed to do—I called her the next day, leaving her a message about how much I enjoyed our conversation.

She never called me back.

Six months later, I saw her in a store, walked right up to her, and said, "Hey, how are you?"

She was taken aback that I was so friendly and not bitter about her never calling me. So we started talking, and after a moment I looked her right in the eye and asked, "You never called—what was up with that?"

She replied, "Yeah, I'm sorry. I got home, and I was so excited about our conversation that I shared the story with my friend. She told me that it didn't feel right—that you must be a player or something. She planted a seed of doubt in my mind, and the second that happened, I started thinking that everything was too perfect. In life, we're taught not to trust anything that's too good to be true, and you honestly seemed too good to be true. I heard your message, and I wanted to call you so back so bad—but I didn't.

"So then I went to another friend and asked her what to do. She told me that I *should* call you back. I was so conflicted. I was just about to go find your number when my other friend called and reminded me about the time that a similar situation occurred where all the guy wanted to do was sleep with me. So a day turned into a week, a week turned into two weeks . . . and I almost dialed your number so many times, but just couldn't do it. I'm sorry."

I had to laugh. "It's funny, isn't it? When we get exactly what we want in life, we don't trust it, because we allow other people—people who weren't there and didn't experience that moment—to ruin it for us," I told her. "You weren't living by your rules, you were living by someone else's."

This woman and I never got together, yet it really didn't matter. It was a great lesson for both of us.

Every time I do one of my boot camps, I remind the guys, "You have to live by your rules, because you only have one shot at this thing called life—one shot to date the people you need to date, one shot to be with the type of person you need to be with. So why hold yourself back by allowing other voices to fill your head when your heart is aching to give you the life you were meant to have? And that's the beauty of life: you can craft it, do what you want, and not have to be anybody else. That's what this journey is all about."

■ ■ ■

Here's a wonderful exercise for you to do right now. Create your own rule book. In it, write down everything that you want to live by—everything that you stand for.

Next, list the rules that other people have given you. Now look at these items, and cross out each one of them. You're not going to live your life according to someone else's rules ever again.

Another exercise is to focus on surrounding yourself with positive, like-minded people. Eliminate anyone from your life who's negative or brings you down. If it's a family member, and he or she starts talking negatively about some of the things that you're experiencing or doing, say, "Oops! I just pulled into my garage, and you're breaking up. Can I call you later? Love you!" If you've got friends who don't support you in your journey to meet somebody fantastic, you need to eliminate them from your life. You can keep them as a friend by e-mailing or talking on the phone once in a while, but the second they try to dominate or control things that are going on with you, you need to hang up.

Understand the power of saying no, because your ability to do so is going to become your best asset. So when a buddy calls on Friday night to ask, "Do you want to go out tonight? We're going to go out all night and party our heads off," you know that this option isn't going to yield the results you want (finding a great mate). So what should you say?

"No."

You can add, "I don't want to. I'd rather do my own thing tonight. I want to go to a tasting at a new restaurant and spend the evening talking to people about gourmet food," "I'm going to go hang out at the coffeehouse," or "I'm going for a swim in the pool." Whatever it is you want to do, do it. Learn to say no. Live by your own rules, because this is *your* life and you're going to run it using *your* rule book. Starting with this moment, stand up and fight for yourself. Right now, go to the mirror, look yourself in the eye, and say, "I'm going to stand up. I'm going to fight for myself. I'm going to meet the best available people for me. And if someone isn't interested, I'm not going to let it bother me. I'm just going to understand that this person doesn't deserve the fantastic individual that I am."

Starting today, I want you to live by your rules and your rules only. You're going to love and honor yourself, and you're going to love and honor every decision you make, whether it's right or wrong. Every judgment you make is the right one so long as you're the one who made it and you trusted yourself when you did so. A total stranger sitting next to you on the subway could be your next great lover, your next great relationship. Don't let someone else's rules come between the two of you. Live by your rules, and your rules only.

Write your rule book, and then live it.

■ ■ ■

AFTERWORD

Let's Get Naked Together

How does it feel to be naked? How does it feel to be totally stripped down to the core of who you are? Does it feel exhilarating? Does it feel life changing? Do you want to head out the door and streak through your neighborhood, just like they did in the '70s? Are you ready to go out there and connect with the world in ways that you never have before?

You may have noticed something throughout this book—I got naked *with* you.

I know that sounds funny, especially if you've been reading in bed. You might even have pictured me sitting naked next to you and had a chuckle. I know I did. But I did get naked, and I got vulnerable along with each person who's picked up this book.

The reason I did that is because life is an evolving, changing, and growing cycle. Every day I need to get naked and challenge myself more. Every day I need to strip down and confront my own fears and work through them. Getting down to my own core is the only way I can live.

The other day I was on the phone with a client, who asked me, "David, I've been doing this 'personal growth' thing for a year. When is my life going to get better?"

"It already is," I assured him. "You're exactly where you're supposed to be right now. I want you to think about that statement and embrace it."

"I don't understand."

"I said you're exactly where you're supposed to be in your life at this moment. Personal growth is a lifelong process—not a one-stop shopping trip. It's not something that happens overnight, or in a week or a month. Take a look at photos of yourself when you were a newborn. Then look at yourself when you were six months old, a year, two years, three years, and so on. Look at how you've changed and evolved in each stage of your life, from birth all the way up to the present moment. Do you notice how different you used to look? Now consider how you thought in each of those years, and how differently you felt."

Like my client, you're on a journey to becoming more naked, open, and vulnerable to the world; and self-growth is going to happen at whatever pace that's meant for you. Some people grow and mature more quickly than others. You may not need to go through the exercises I've included more than once, or you might need to do them several times before they stick. Everyone is unique, and whatever works best for you is what you should do.

While we're talking about the exercises, I want you to take a few minutes to look through the entire book. Which exercises did you successfully complete, and which ones do you need to do over again? This is really important.

When I became fully naked myself, sometimes I needed to go through exercises 10, 11, and 12 or more times. The reality is that some lessons are harder to learn than others, and some habits and fears are more difficult to overcome than others. You probably breezed right through some of the tasks I asked you to complete, since they were easy for you. They were things you might have been working on before, and this was just validation and confirmation for you. Others might have been more challenging. This isn't a problem—it's not a big deal at all. Simply go back and do them until you're happy with the results.

Remember: personal growth is a lifelong process.

Just because there are only a few more pages left doesn't mean that you're done with the work that you need to do in order to find the perfect mate. It's not enough that you've gotten naked with me—you need to *stay* naked. To accomplish this, you need to go out there and apply all of the things you've learned over and over again so you can get a bit closer to mastering this part of your life once and for all.

Love is amazing and grand, but in order to find Mr. or Ms. Right, you need to first love every bit of *yourself.*

I don't want you to move forward with your relationships in frustration. I don't want you to bang your head against the wall because your partner doesn't understand you sexually or emotionally. The only reason why this would ever happen again is because you aren't being honest with yourself and didn't do the exercises I've provided.

After reading this book, completing the exercises, and putting my recommendations into practice, you should never have another disappointing intimate relationship again. The conversations you have with the next person you fall in love with should flow easily and freely, because you know that you need to be with somebody who is a great communicator. You know you need to be with a person who expresses his or her feelings, because, if you've done everything I've asked of you honestly and to the best of your ability, the tools I've given you will have opened up your true self.

You now realize that life is full of abundance, so you don't need to settle for a mate who's going to frustrate you. It's awful to be on that treadmill, knowing that you need to jump off. How many times have you been in a relationship and given somebody your blueprint—a detailed look at your needs and desires—only to have them ignore or stomp on it?

We all give away our blueprints, especially after we become naked. We become totally open and comfortable enough to communicate everything we need: "Look, babe, I really love it when you rub my head. It feels so good. Can you do it more often?" "I love when we make love for two hours a day. Let's plan to do that a few days a week. It makes me feel so wonderful," or "It's so nice when you just call me in the middle of the day to express yourself with beauty and vulnerability."

And when your partners don't do any of those things after you've revealed your deepest feelings, it can drive you crazy. You've opened up to them and given them your blueprint. The problem is that they're not taking it in, they're not embracing it, and they haven't learned the key to love.

Always show love the way you know how; but to really love someone, do so in the way your mate needs. *That's* true love.

By doing that, you've dropped your own ego, embraced who you are, and accepted your good qualities along with the bad. You're working on the things that you want to change, and you're allowing yourself time to grow and blossom. And then when you meet some-body special, you'll naturally want to love this person in the way he or she longs for.

■ ■ ■

Isn't it a beautiful thing to be involved in a relation-ship where you're able to satisfy the other person's needs after they've been revealed to you? It means that you really love yourself and expect nothing back in return. And when you get to this level of giving selflessly, you're always going to receive the love you require tenfold.

Life is a miracle. And people who have become total-ly naked are 100 percent vulnerable—and 100 percent okay with everything that happens as a result of their vulnerability. You become the most attractive, amazing, and beautiful person you're meant to be.

What's the deepest truth you learned from the infor-mation I've given you? In fact, here's one last exercise: I want you to write the biggest "aha!" moment you had while reading *Naked!* What triggered that thought?

Next, I want you to share the book with as many people as you can. I ask this because, if you think about it, if everybody stripped down naked, how much easier would it be to live in this world?

It's almost like magic pixie dust that we're talking about here. By becoming naked, all of us together will be seeking out—and eventually find—the answers to life's biggest questions.

When I'm going through some sort of problem, guess how I solve it? I get 100 percent naked. I might be sitting in my living room or driving my car when I suddenly think to myself, *What's bothering me right now? What do I need to learn? What lesson am I looking for?*

And what do I do in that situation? I go out and seek answers.

But wait—I don't go to my friends for answers. They know me really, really well, and always tend to take my side. I search for what I'm looking for in the world at large, because this planet contains all the answers I seek—and everything *you* could ever want or need as well. If you're really in tune with who you are, you're going to find others in the same situation as you—those who are seeking answers, too, and want to talk. And you'll be able to communicate who you are and get a real sense of your own vulnerability. Simply by getting naked, you'll find the support of all the individuals out there who are willing and able to connect with you.

Basically, when you start working through things, you're going to find other people who are on the same path. You may even run into somebody in your local supermarket and get into the most intense conversation, because that's who you need to meet that day. It's really amazing to be able to do this on a regular basis; after all, you're on this planet right now to connect with, embrace, and get naked with others. All of the answers are right in front of you, within your grasp. All you've got to do is get out of your head and into your heart and the world around you. Once you do that, you'll have more dates, more friends than you know what to do with, and some of the most amazingly intimate experiences that so far you've only dreamed of.

How do I know this? Because everything that I've written about I've done for myself, and I continue to do every day whenever I need to look deep inside. Like you, I desired to have the most incredible, amazing love life, and I was able to accomplish that by doing everything in this book.

■ ■ ■

Thank you for getting naked with me, thank you for allowing me to share my thoughts with you, and thank you for sharing everything with me in return. I put my passion into these pages, and I know all of you feel it.

I look forward to meeting you in the future at one of my seminars, or maybe just out and about. If you ever see me on the street, in a lobby of a hotel, or on an airplane, come over and introduce yourself and tell me how the book impacted you—how you felt about it afterward, and how it changed your dating life. Feel free to send me an e-mail anytime to tell me about your successes, because the more you reach out to me, the more I learn and the more I connect with you.

From the bottom of my heart, thank you for reading *Naked!* and best wishes on the journey that is your life.

■ ■ ■

ACKNOWLEDGMENTS

I wasn't alone in bringing this book to fruition, and I would like to take this opportunity to thank everyone who helped along the way. First, I'd like to thank my dog, Daphne, for helping out at all the boot camps (if you've ever attended one, you'll know what I mean). I'd also like to thank Bryan Swerling—my co-author on my first book, *Always Talk to Strangers*—for his continuing friendship and support. I'd also like to thank Peter Economy for his writing support on this project; and my literary agent, Michael Ebeling, for hounding me for years to take this book from a vision to reality. Thanks also to my wife, Sonja, for giving me the space to write; and to my daughter, Layla, for helping me understand what being a father is all about. And last but not least, thank you to every client I've ever worked with. Without you, I wouldn't be where I am today.

■ ■ ■

ABOUT THE AUTHOR

David Wygant is an internationally renowned dating and relationship coach, author, and speaker. Over the last 20 years, he has become one of the most frequently quoted dating experts in the media. He writes for *The Huffington Post* and **www.AskMen.com**; and offers his advice via numerous communication outlets. David's website, **www.davidwygant.com**, is a popular resource for singles, and he can frequently be found there blogging.

David's clientele ranges from everyday people to professional athletes, top business executives, and celebrities. He is a dynamic visual presence, and has been called upon for his unique skills by an impressive list of domestic and international television shows and networks. Some of the many media appearances he has made include: E!, *Starting Over, Party @ The Palms,* ABC News, CBS's *The Early Show,* MTV *(Sex2k* and *Made),* The Learning Channel (TLC), BBC, Playboy TV, UPN, The WB, *Blind Date, Starting Over,* Comcast Network, National

Enquirer, Blitz TV (Germany), and *A Current Affair* (Australia).

David is a ubiquitous presence in the print media, including major publications such as the *Los Angeles Times, Daily Herald, The Dallas Morning News, The Miami Herald, The Boston Globe, The Philadelphia Inquirer, Marie Claire, New York* magazine, *Figure, Harper's Bazaar, Maxim, Cosmopolitan,* **Match.com**, and many more.

During the course of his career, David Wygant has made guest appearances on more than 2,000 radio shows. His voice and words have profoundly touched the lives of many people in every major U.S. city, as well as in many medium- and small-sized cities.

David's speaking programs, workshops, and seminars are in great demand around the world. His three-day Group Bootcamps are offered in the largest markets—including New York City, Los Angeles, and London—and his hourly coaching and exclusive one-on-one programs are extremely popular. Additionally, his *Men's Mastery Series* and *Women's Mastery Series* are the most comprehensive home-study resources for dating coaching available anywhere.

In 2005, David wrote the popular book *Always Talk to Strangers: 3 Simple Steps to Finding the Love of Your Life* (Perigee/Penguin), which maintained a top-100 ranking on Amazon for several weeks.

■ ■ ■

NOTES

NOTES

NOTES

Hay House Titles of Related Interest

We hope you enjoyed this Hay House book. If you'd like to receive our online catalog featuring additional information on Hay House books and products, or if you'd like to find out more about the Hay Foundation, please contact:

Hay House, Inc., P.O. Box 5100, Carlsbad, CA 92018-5100
(760) 431-7695 or (800) 654-5126
(760) 431-6948 (fax) or (800) 650-5115 (fax)
www.hayhouse.com® • **www.hayfoundation.org**

■ ■ ■

Published and distributed in Australia by:
Hay House Australia Pty. Ltd., 18/36 Ralph St., Alexandria NSW 2015
Phone: 612-9669-4299 • *Fax:* 612-9669-4144 • www.hayhouse.com.au

Published and distributed in the United Kingdom by:
Hay House UK, Ltd., 292B Kensal Rd., London W10 5BE • *Phone:*
44-20-8962-1230 • *Fax:* 44-20-8962-1239 • www.hayhouse.co.uk

Published and distributed in the Republic of South Africa by:
Hay House SA (Pty), Ltd., P.O. Box 990, Witkoppen 2068
Phone/Fax: 27-11-467-8904 • www.hayhouse.co.za

Published in India by: Hay House Publishers India, Muskaan
Complex, Plot No. 3, B-2, Vasant Kunj, New Delhi 110 070 • *Phone:*
91-11-4176-1620 • *Fax:* 91-11-4176-1630 • www.hayhouse.co.in

Distributed in Canada by:
Raincoast, 9050 Shaughnessy St., Vancouver, B.C. V6P 6E5
Phone: (604) 323-7100 • *Fax:* (604) 323-2600 • www.raincoast.com

■ ■ ■

Take Your Soul on a Vacation

Visit **www.HealYourLife.com®** to regroup, recharge, and reconnect with your own magnificence.Featuring blogs, mind-body-spirit news, and life-changing wisdom from Louise Hay and friends.

Visit **www.HealYourLife.com** today!

Lightning Source UK Ltd.
Milton Keynes UK
UKOW042129070313

207288UK00001B/96/P